Victory Over The Gates: Restoring A Soul From Captivity

by Sywithia Todd

Edited by Edith Houghton

ISBN-13: 979-8-234-04483-9

ISBN-13: 979-8-234-06951-1

Printed in the United States of America

Unless otherwise indicated, all Scripture quotations are taken from the King James Version of the Bible. Used by permission.

CONTENTS

Foreword 1

Introduction 5

1. Breaking through the Territorial Gate 7
2. Before the War 15
3. The War with the Gates of Hell Begins 27
4. Dealing with the Family Gate 33
5. Breaking through the Gate of Comfort 39
6. Breaking through the Gate of Comfort – Part 2 43
7. The Eye and Ear Gates 47
8. Who are the Demonic Gatekeepers? 53
9. Help Against the Gates 57
10. God's Protection Against the Gates 61
11. Revelation of the Gates 69
12. Rest from the Fight 79
13. Understanding the Real Battle 85
14. The Dream Gate 89
15. Generational Gates 93

16. The Root of the Problem 97

17. The End-Times Connection 101

18. The Legal Right 105

19. The Gate of Entertainment 111

20. The Dots Finally Connect 115

21. The Warfare Afterwards 121

Afterword 127

STAY CONNECTED 131

FOREWORD

We have to be careful concerning the information which we allow to enter our temple (our body). The Bible tells us to guard our gates in numerous scriptures (Matthew 6:22-23, Proverbs 4:20-23 and Psalm 141:3). We need to be especially vigilant as to what we entertain in our minds because that is where the real spiritual battlefield is found. The enemy of our souls knows that the only way to produce an action that is contrary to what God's best intentions for us are, is by getting us to entertain a thought that is contrary to God's kingdom, the kingdom of light. It is only after thinking about something that action will follow. When Adam and Eve broke relationship with God by choosing to pursue knowledge rather than the life-giving relationship that only God offers by consuming the fruit of the tree of the knowledge of good and evil, they failed in guarding their gates. They chose to make knowledge and the pursuit of knowledge their "god" rather than trusting in God Almighty who had very explicitly warned them that on the day when they consumed from the tree of the knowledge of good and evil, surely they would die. Up until that point they did not know or even begin to comprehend what death was. The Bible tells us in numerous places that the wages of sin is death (Romans 6:23); what this means is that when we choose to sin, our spirit becomes even farther separated from God and actually experiences death.

The most important question to ask when considering new information is actually a twofold question: what does this mean, and what must I do? It's vital to sit with the Lord and consider that question concerning the things that we choose to ingest. One might ask, "why do I need to read this book," or "why is this information important to me and my life?" One reason is that because knowledge once breathed upon by the Lord becomes revelation. When that occurs, the revelation which we receive has the capacity to impact our heart and becomes a part of our experience. When something becomes a part of our experience, it has the capacity to transform us which is why the Bible tells us to no longer try to conform ourselves to the world, but rather to be transformed by the renewing of our minds (Romans 12:2). As we are transformed, we begin to understand who it is that God has actually made us to be and that allows us to step into alignment with God's plans and purposes for our life. As we grow in understanding what our true identity is, eventually that identity will burst forth out of us creating an atmosphere around us which is known as presence. Jesus told the woman at the well and others that once they drank of the living water that only He could provide, that same water would burst forth from their bellies and others would be able to drink from it (John 4 and John 7:38). When someone actually knows who it is that they are and who it is that they were made to be and what their purpose is, that essence actually precedes them and is capable of shifting the spiritual atmosphere wherever they are present. Jesus is a very clear example of this phenomenon - His presence provoked people in a mighty way.

As ministers of reconciliation and ambassadors for the kingdom of God, we need to learn how to walk in the authority that Jesus has given us. In the Bible Jesus told His disciples that they were to serve as the light of the world and He then commissioned them to go out and cast out demons, raise the dead, heal the sick and set free the oppressed (Matthew 10:1-8 and 28:16-20, Mark 16:15-18). We are to bring the light of the kingdom of God wherever we go and to shine it brightly, especially in situations where the darkness has gone unchecked. We are to continue to advance the kingdom of God wherever we go and there will be clashes with the kingdom of darkness as we enforce what Jesus accomplished on the cross. Jesus was asked what the end of the age would look like by His disciples and He commented that those days would look just as it had looked in the days of Noah. For far too long the church has neglected to consider or address that particular admonition. We tend to look on things in a euphemistic way rather than actually digging deeper and considering what does that really mean? In the days of Noah there was incredible evil going on throughout the world. Sexual sin was rampant and the watcher Angels had given mankind access to knowledge that they were never supposed to have. Some examples of this forbidden knowledge included, but are not limited to: astrology, alchemy, and warfare. The watcher Angels had actually traded this information to the sons of men who were willing to give their daughters through the covenant of marriage to those "fallen angels". The rampant evil present on the face of the earth actually caused God to flood the entire earth in order to eradicate the corrupted bloodline that had been developed through the intermingling of the watcher angels and the daughters of men. The Bible tells us that those angels were sequestered in hell, a place made specifically for them and are chained there until the final Judgement (Jude 1:6 and 2 Peter 2:4).

I believe that one of the things that we are going to need to do as Christians during these “End Times” is to understand the authority that we walk in because of what Jesus accomplished on the cross as He overcame the world and took back the keys from Satan and led captivity captive. In order to be able to succeed and walk in dominion during these End Times, we need to understand what it is that we're up against. We also need to understand that it is a spiritual battle and that in the name of Jesus we already have the victory. Remember, we overcome by the blood of the Lamb, and by the word of our testimony, and not loving our lives unto death (Revelation 12:11).

By Edith Houghton

INTRODUCTION

I am writing this book to reveal truth and to lead others into a deeper understanding of what to bring before God in prayer. The "gates of hell" devised a plan to get me out of the way to destroy my family and any other souls who would be directly impacted by my obedience as I fulfill the divine purpose for my life. Although God tried to warn me ahead of time, I only truly understood the warning once harm had already occurred. Consider this snapshot testimony of my life as a warning to expose the enemy's tactics which I experienced.

"And I say also unto thee, That thou art Peter, and upon this rock I will build my church; and the gates of hell shall not prevail against it. And I will give unto thee the keys of the kingdom of heaven: and whatsoever thou shalt bind on earth shall be bound in heaven: and whatsoever thou shalt loose on earth shall be loosed in heaven. Then charged he his disciples that they should tell no man that he was Jesus the Christ." (Matthew 16:18-20, KJV)

Prayer

I pray that you are covered by the Blood of Jesus Christ as you read this book. Jesus, let the life of the person reading this book never be the same. I pray that your plans for their life come to pass. Let every child connected to their life escape the traps of the devil. Let no weapon formed against them or their families prosper in the mighty name of

Jesus. The gates of hell will not prevail against your life. Let there be no fear but the Fear of the Lord Jesus. Shine a light on every dark and hidden place. Expose everything that was hidden by the devil to entrap them and their family. Set every captive free!

In Jesus mighty name. Amen!

Chapter One

Breaking Through the Territorial Gate

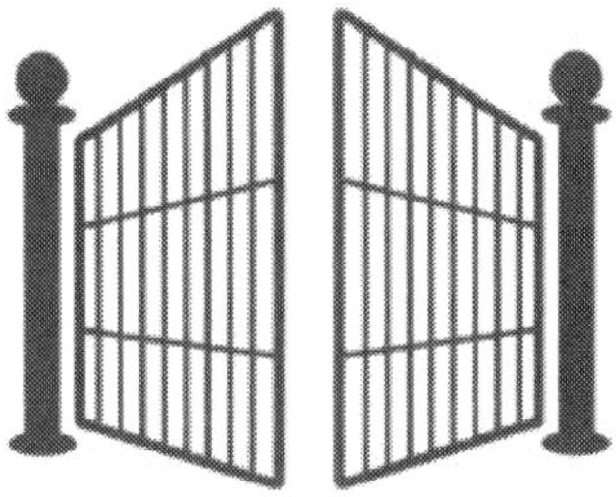

In my dream, I was surrounded by several gargoyle looking, evil beings with wings. As I was going straight up in the air, we were fighting. If someone was to see that battle, they would have said it was a tie. The demonic beings were fighting me all the way as I traveled upwards. Then I heard a peaceful, audible voice telling me to get up. I woke up fully alert out of that dream. I woke up to peace, which was strange, given the dream I just had. This was the first time I heard the audible voice of God! I had no fear while in the dream or afterwards. God did not give us a spirit of fear, but of power, love, and a sound mind (2 Timothy 1:7). When you truly understand that you are in the hands of Jesus, what do you have to fear?

In the dream, I was fighting demonic beings like they were human. I was throwing punches and kicks. That was the problem. That is why I was not winning the fight and God told me to "get up". In other words, come up higher. We cannot win the fight against demonic entities unless we fight with God's weapons and take our seat in heavenly places (Ephesians 2:6). This is far above principalities. From the position of heavenly places, they are under our feet. Our weapons are not carnal, but mighty through God for the pulling down of strongholds (2 Corinthians 10:4). We wrestle not against flesh and blood, but against principalities, powers, the rulers of darkness of this world, and spiritual wickedness in high places (Ephesians 6:12). The wings on the beings led me to believe they were principalities or powers.

Shortly after that dream God told me to leave St. Louis. It was a fight to move out of St. Louis. On the day of the move, they no longer wanted to move my belongings for the agreed upon price. They wanted to increase the amount by almost $500. That was $500 that I did not have to give yet. After an hour of being on the phone with the company that set it up, they decided to go ahead and move my belongings. A couple of years later, my sister faced even more difficulties when it came time for her to move - on her moving day, the mover did not even show up.

Apparently, those territorial gatekeepers did not want to lose me as their prisoner. My move was the key to fulfilling my purpose, calling, and destiny. When we succeed in learning who we were made and begin to move into our divine purpose, it hurts the kingdom of darkness. For instance, Abram's move from Ur of the Chaldees towards the promised land blessed the nations. It was God that told Abram to leave. Have you ever noticed that a lot of people say they want to move, only to be saying the same thing ten years later? These people are bound. Deep down, they know that divine purpose is attached to their leaving that city, but there is a fight to get out. For some, the fight is financial, their family, or fear of the unknown, as well as lies of the enemy. For some, God has purposed for them to stay where they are living when they begin living their lives for Him. Whether you stay or leave, there is still spiritual warfare.

Territory is any area of land under the jurisdiction of a ruler. This territory can be large or small. On a smaller scale, it is home and/or land ownership. On a larger scale, it is states, nations, and empires. An empire is comprised of multiple nations under one rule. The principality that enforces Islam rules multiple nations. That principality has established a demonic empire under a false anti-Christ religion that has multiple nations bound.

The more believers in Jesus Christ that own houses and land, the more it becomes a blessing to the community. When multiple believers' own properties and businesses, it is a territorial victory for the kingdom of heaven. The rulers of darkness of this world fight hard to keep money and land out of the hands of believers. Therefore, taking physical territory is also spiritual warfare, and business in general is spiritual warfare. You must go through the gatekeepers to enter the corporate world. Oftentimes people go to a specific school to study a particular subject only to not succeed when they try to break into their field of choice. I experienced a lot of resistance as I tried to get a corporate job.

The devil does not want any money to get into the hands of those who are not serving him. For those that are making a difference within the Kingdom of God or having a positive impact on the generations of their family, it is a war. It took me lots of direction from God along with much prayer and fasting for me to break through one of the gates. There are territorial gatekeepers ruling over some corporations. When I finally entered the corporate world, I learned that just a few companies own most of the businesses. There are fortified walls around those corporations, much like the walls around old cities, preventing believers from accessing their wealth. Cities in ancient times were often surrounded by walls, and access was possible only through gates. The walls of Jericho protected their city from outside intruders. We know what happened to Jericho's walls when the people praised God (Joshua Chapter 6). Those territorial walls fell when the Israelites obeyed God's instructions. The gates in the walls of a city controlled who could come in and who could go out of the city. Soldiers guarded each gate and admitted only certain individuals. Enemies could not go through the gate without using force. The kingdom of heaven suffers violence, and the violent take it by force (Matthew 11:12). The gateways of the kingdoms of both light and darkness are guarded by gatekeepers. The gatekeepers in our fallen world are the principalities, powers, rulers of darkness, and spiritual wickedness in high places.

One of the principalities over my hometown of St. Louis promotes delay and stagnation. In St. Louis, my finances and destiny seemed to be stagnant. God told me years ago, to get away from family and to move out of St. Louis. The Holy Spirit led me to read the account of Abraham as confirmation. God told Abram to get out of his country and away from his family. Abram's father's name was Terah. Terah means delay or wanderer or station. This was God telling Abram to get away from a place of delay and stagnation. Do not make any place your station when God has told you to move away from it.

The Lord Jesus commissioned believers to go throughout all the world and preach the gospel to every creature (Mark 16:15). Why did Jesus say the world? The world is the whole earth, people, and all its places. The whole world was not just the nations. It means taking territory and establishing dominion over the air, the land, and the sea. Preaching the gospel to "the whole creation" (Mark 16:15, ESV) is not just for humans, this is for all of God's creation that is on the earth. This does not mean the salvation of all the creation but a proclamation that all creation must bow to the good news of Jesus Christ. This means all the demons, principalities, rulers of darkness of this world, and spiritual wickedness in high places must move out of the way when we proclaim the gospel of Jesus Christ. They must move out of the way for people to receive the good news of salvation; they cannot stop people from choosing to receive salvation through their free will. Salvation is only for humans, or those that came out of Adam and Eve.

are some places that are no longer ruled by demonic principalities even if the area still has demonic activities occurring. In those places, revival flows freely with little resistance. The principalities in those regions have been moved out of the way by the kingdom of heaven. God's angelic army is still fighting to establish God's kingdom within the earth. It is the believer's job to continue to commission God's army by putting voice to the Word of God. By doing that, we take territory for God by force.

Territories have gateways. The St. Louis Arch is an iconic symbol known as the "Gateway to the West." The arch was possibly built on and is within ten minutes from Native American mounds. Mounds were flat-topped pyramid structures built as burial, ceremonial, and ritual sites. In other words, the mounds were places where demonic altars were established to demonic deities. Instead of tearing them down and dedicating that territory to the Lord Jesus Christ, we have allowed them to remain today.

A list of the mounds along with the meaning of their names and their locations:

- **Cahokia** (wild geese) Collinsville, Illinois (close to St. Louis, MO)
- **Effigy** (a crude image of a person or an idol) Harpers Ferry, Iowa
- **Etowah, (**an important town Cartersville, Georgia
- **Watson Brake** Logtown, Louisiana
- **Poverty Point** (a state of being extremely poor) Poverty Point, Louisiana
- **Serpent Mound** Peebles, Ohio
- **Pinson** (pinch) Pinson, Tennessee
- **Observatory Hill Mounds** (a high place to observe the stars) Madison, Wisconsin
- **Spiro Mounds**("spirit") Spiro, Oklahoma
- **Moundville** (village of burial site) Moundville, Alabama

The names of the mounds give clues as to what type of warfare to expect in those territories. It is not just the mound name which gives clues, but also the landmarks that are set up in proximity to it. The territorial spirits which rule over these areas are part of the gates of hell and the kingdom of darkness. We need to understand that some battles are not only generational but are also territorial. We overcome all these battles by the blood of the Lamb which Jesus Christ willingly shed for our victory while on the cross.

There are also areas in the United States of America that have been re-established as territories for the Lord Jesus Christ. Some of these locations are called prayer mountains. You can see the difference in those territories when compared to the other places within the United States. For instance, both Dallas, Texas and Moravian Falls, North Carolina have established prayer mountains. These mountains are known locations where people go to spend time with the Lord in prayer. There were major differences which I noticed between St. Louis and Dallas when I finally got there. Dallas has a mega-church on almost every corned while it seemed that church growth in St. Louis was stagnant.

Geographical regions have gateways which provide access or entrance through an opening in a wall or fence. The spiritual being that is in authority over a given region will establish gatekeepers to limit access to their region. These ruling powers want to maintain control over their regions as well as dictate the atmosphere within these areas. They also strive to protect the high places and/or altars which have been used to worship them. When Jacob laid his head upon a rock and fell asleep in the wilderness, he had a dream in which he saw the angels ascending and descending (Genesis 28:16-18). He had discovered a gate of heaven, so he used the stone as a pillar (or monument to his experience) and poured oil upon the top of that location. The Hebrew word, ***maṣ·ṣê·ḇāh***, used for pillar, means a memorial. The gate that Jacob discovered was an altar which had been established by Abraham years earlier. The gate allowed the angels to ascend and descend from heaven and actually created an open heaven there over that area.

God told the Israelites to destroy the altars, break the images of any idols, and cut down their groves (Exodus 34:13) when the Israelites were taking territory as they travelled through the wilderness on their way to the promised land. There are high places and altars like these throughout the United States. These areas should be either torn down or re-dedicated to the Lord Jesus Christ. I believe this is one reason it is hard for revival to be birthed in Saint Louis and the churches in that region remain stagnant. To this day there is demonic oppression over that city, as well as active witchcraft. There are other major cities within the United States which have the same issues.

The intriguing thing is that Africa is known for witchcraft, however, witchcraft and occultism in the US arc far more prevalent than most

Americans understand. When I see the word "gate", I immediately think about a portal and gateway to hell. When considering the "Gateway to the West" located in St. Louis, I find myself wondering what exactly is coming through those gates? In a vision, a friend of mine saw Nephilim coming through the Gateway Arch. I will explain what Nephilim are in greater detail later. That vision could explain why there is so much crime and murder within the city of St. Louis. According to U.S. News & World Report, St. Louis is ranked #3 on the lists of Most Dangerous Places in the U.S. in 2025 to 2026 .

As Christians, we have weapons, but we need to know where to aim them in unison as the Body of Christ. We need to aim our spiritual weapons against the territorial gates. Our spiritual weapons can be found by reading the Holy Bible. Warning: this type of warfare should not be done alone; this type of warfare should be done corporately.

God used my experiences to awaken the prayer warrior on the inside of me. Follow my journey until the end and you will find out why it was so critical for me to break through the territorial gate. Hopefully, you will learn something that will help you walk in a greater level of authority as you read about my personal spiritual battle with the gates of hell.

CHAPTER TWO

BEFORE THE WAR

I was living alone in my one-bedroom apartment in St. Louis, Missouri. It was so quiet and peaceful. As I lay down on the bed, I looked up at the ceiling. After ten years of waiting, I wondered if God had forgotten about me. Was I meant to be single and/or childless? When was I going to meet my husband? Does he live in another state or even another county? I could hear no answer. I fell into a deep sleep when I should have been praying. Before dawn, my spirit woke up. While still in a state of being half asleep and half awake, I heard a conversation coming out of the bathroom. It was three spirits discussing me. One of them said, "I thought you said she is here. I do not see her." Another one said, "There she is." The three evil spirits moved towards my bedroom. I somehow fell back asleep. Sometime later my body sat straight up, and I went into a night vision. In the vision, I saw a large snake as big as the ceiling flying in my room. I immediately woke up out of my sleep, praying. After I finished praying, I got ready for work and headed out the door.

As I arrived at work, I went through security. The security there looks like they could easily work for the Secret Service. I know that where I work is a major corporation, but why are they treating this place like the White House? The security was on the roof top with black suits, shades, and earpieces in their ears. The first day on this job felt as if I were walking straight into a government building. I needed to swipe my badge to enter the garage, to get past the security desk, and again to get onto certain floors. It quickly became clear that I would not be getting breakfast this morning from the cafeteria, so I headed straight for the elevator. Something felt off that day. I noticed that a lot of my co-workers were out of the office today. I decided to go into the breakroom to get coffee. My coworker who was from China entered the breakroom. "Good morning, Chia," I greeted her. "Good morning, Sy," she said, and then asked, "Have you been watching the news?" I said, "No." She said, "COVID is getting bad, and half the team is out sick today. I talked to my family in China, and it is really bad over there. I am going to work from home tomorrow." I said, "I did not think COVID was that bad." Chia said, "No Sy, it is. I have family close to the region of the outbreak." Since Chia said she would be working from home, I took the option to work from home as well. Although COVID was evil, God actually used it as a way for me to eventually leave St. Louis.

Well, what started to be days turned into weeks and then weeks turned into months. I was still working from home, thinking "God help me. I am in the middle of a pandemic, and You still have not sent my husband. How am I going to meet him now?" A friend suggested that I try online dating to which I responded, "Absolutely not." I thought to myself there cannot be any saved men online. However, it was too late, a seed was planted. I did not hold on to what God told me. After thinking about it for a while, I thought to myself, "What if you are holding yourself back? God can use anything. Well, let me try it out." I started online dating.

After a week in, I realized it's a jungle with online dating. It is like being in a pool surrounded by sharks. I was done! I was about to deactivate my account when a man whose profile said he was a Christian, liked my profile. I viewed his profile, and he seemed normal. I liked his profile. He messaged me and said he wanted to video chat outside of the online dating platform. The man was attractive, charming, and had a sense of humor. So, I agreed. After the first video conversation, I heard within my spirit, "You are unequally yoked." I said to myself, "let me cut this off." The man then asked, "Can I call you again?" He preferred video chatting. I said, "I would rather video chat, but I will be extremely busy this weekend. Plus, I think we are unequally yoked." He began to talk about the bible and said that he led a service once. I decided to keep going forward because of my desire to be married.

I continued to talk to this man. We talked every day for about an hour. On one video call, I noticed that his T-Shirt had a snake on it with the phrase "Strike First. Strike Hard. No Mercy." At that time in my life, I did not trust my discernment. Prior to meeting him, I'd had a vision of a large snake coming at me. Although there were obvious signs, I dismissed them as being self-sabotage; I put them off to my being in uncertain, new territory. He said he wanted to meet me in person. I was not ready for that. I hesitated, but I finally let him convince me and I agreed to meet him in person.

He flew me out first-class to visit him for a week in Seattle, Washington. While on the flight from Saint Louis to Seattle, I thought to myself, 'you are on a first-class ticket to hell.' I felt no peace at all, yet I still dismissed it as self-sabotage. Later, I discovered that I had discerned the situation correctly; this was a setup, organized to bring destruction into my life and get me out of the way so that the plans of the kingdom of darkness could succeed.

When I arrived at the Seattle airport, he was waiting for me at the baggage claim inside the airport. I was surprised to see him sitting there. I had wanted to talk to my friends on the phone for a bit longer before he got there and I met him. We walked out of the airport into the garage. He put my suitcase into the trunk of his black car which had dark tinted windows. I asked him to take me to the hotel. He dropped me off at the Sheraton hotel, saying, "we will talk later." When I called him, he told me that I had "disrespected him." According to him, it was disrespectful for me to get a hotel when he had fixed up a room for me at his house. I was certain that I had told him that I had booked a hotel room. At that very moment, I seriously began to question myself. I began to reason within my mind: he had booked my flight; he is right, I was being disrespectful. I felt guilty because he purchased my plane ticket and prepared his place for me. There was no reason for that guilt, yet I had it. I canceled my hotel room and went to his place. He commented to me, "Do you want to get married or are you trying to be Paulina?" At the time, I took that reference to me trying to be like Paul as a negative thing. Now, I can only hope to be used in the same way that God used Paul.

When I arrived at his place, I had no peace. I dismissed it as being nervous. I started looking around the place. He showed me the separate bedroom that he had set up for me. I looked in the closet; I saw mostly military uniforms. His place was neat and clean. I looked at his bookshelf in the living room. There were three books that got my attention. One book was The Battlefield of the Mind, written by Joyce Meyers. The second book was about spiritual abuse and the last one was about how to read body language. He left me in his place alone while he went to get me something to eat. I looked up in the living room, towards the kitchen and I saw a statue of a dragon. He came back with my food and after I ate, I headed for bed.

I woke up around 1 AM and heard a strange noise coming from the living room. I got up to check it out. It was him in front of the computer playing a video game called "Warcraft". He looked at me with a smirk, and said, "You are probably thinking, what in the devil worship is going on?" Then, he laughed. I played it off and went back to bed. I found myself wondering whether this man was joking or serious? Why did he say, "devil worship"? I found out later that game was not just a video game. It was an occultic and demonic video game. Many of these video games are not just for entertainment. At that time, however, I was an ignorant church-going only Christian. Since then, I have learned that witches and warlocks also go to church. I have even met some so-called Christian witches.

The next day, I stepped into his bedroom. When I looked around, I saw many occultic books. I also saw some freemasonry books, a bible, Islamic books, Illuminati type books, an eye on the pyramid book, and other occultic books. I looked down and saw a masonic symbol on a bag. When he noticed that I was looking around, he said, "I do not like your nosiness. That is not going to work for me. You need to stop that." I then asked him, "Are you a mason?" He proudly said, "Yes." He said, "it is like being in any other fraternity." However, the truth is that all sororities and fraternities are rooted in freemasonry, even the Christian ones as they require the members to make vows and covenants. They all have occultic roots.

For us to truly walk in the authority which Jesus regained for us through his sacrifice on the cross, we need to understand what it means when we take a vow or enter into a covenant through the shedding of blood. The Bible warns us that "my people are destroyed for lack of knowledge" (Hosea 4:6, NKJV). The topic of vows and covenants is one which the church traditionally has not taught on very much.

We are made in the very image of God and when He spoke, things happened - consider the very first chapter of Genesis. The Bible warns us in numerous scriptures that there is power in the tongue, in fact, it states: "death and life *are* in the power of the tongue" (Proverbs 18:21, NKJV). The Bible also warns us that it is impossible for us to tame our tongue (James 3:8) on our own. It is imperative for us to learn how to tame our tongue with the help of the Lord because, just as a rudder steers a ship, so does our tongue influence our actions and the course of our lives (James 3:4-6). When we make a vow, we are actually operating contrary to God's Word which tells us point blank to not make vows (Ecclesiastes 5:2-5 and Matthew 5:33-37) because we do not have the capacity to keep them.

The best example of "cutting a covenant" is provided for us during the story of Abram leaving his family when directed to by God. As can be imagined, after walking hundreds of miles in search of the land that God had promised him while also waiting for the birth of his first child and heir, Abram began to grow discouraged. He openly spoke to God, sharing his concern that he still did not have the land nor did he have a child, and the only thing that he felt was happening was he was getting older, beyond the age where most would already have children. The Lord reassured Abram and told him he was going to establish a covenant between the two of them. He tasked Abram with getting the animals and birds required for the covenant ceremony (Genesis 15:9).

Abram gathered the animals requested by the Lord and prepared them as was customary for establishing a covenant and then he placed the halves of each carcass opposite each other, creating a pathway. This was to signify the idea that even when the covenant partners were walking through the valley of death, surrounded by it on all sides with blood flowing, they would be allies. Those entering into a covenant together would usually exchange weapons and a robe or mantle, and even signet rings, indicating to each other that "my weapons are your weapons and the authority which I have I also grant to you and when you fight, I will fight alongside of you unto death." Abram knew the importance of the covenant which the Lord was calling him to enter into and so after the animals had been cut in half and positioned the Bible tells us he protected the carcasses from scavenger birds until the Lord arrived for the covenant ceremony. The intriguing thing is that the Lord then caused a deep sleep to come over Abram, and instead of Abraham actually walking through the covenant offerings, the Lord walked through it as "a smoking oven and a torch that passed between those pieces." (Genesis 15:17, NKJV) The Lord Himself passed through the covenant pieces in two different manifestations of his presence because he knew the weakness of man and that Abram himself would not be strong enough to hold up his end of the covenant by himself. It is interesting to note that generations later the Lord would show himself as a cloud of smoke by day and a pillar of fire at night as He led the Israelites through the wilderness (Exodus 13:21-22).

When I knew this man was a Mason, I asked him with a serious look on my face, "Why would you join?" He replied, "Why are you judging me?" Then, he turned into a totally different person right before my eyes and the spirit of rage manifested. It was like he went from being Dr. Jekyll to Mr. Hyde. In a rage, he grabbed my suitcase and started heading towards the door. Then, he stopped. I thought he was about to kick me out and leave me stranded, which concerned me. I did not know anyone in Seattle. Instead, he took my stuff into another room.

In the middle of it all, God was still talking to me. God told me, "I am fighting for you." Feeling ashamed and almost dirty for just being there, I said to the Lord, " Jesus, you see my situation, yet you're still fighting for me." God then said, "This is generational." I had not been taught about generational curses. Later in my Christian walk, I learned that patterns in relationships can be connected to generational patterns, curses and even demons.

The man then said, "I am changing your flight and sending you home." At this point, I played it off like I was sad. However, I knew that was God giving me a way of escape. He took me to the airport the next day. As soon as I got home, he called me. He asked, "Why did you leave me?" I said, "You told me to leave." Did he not remember what he said? That was crazy.

We started talking on the phone again. At this point, I must have been under some type of spell. Even after all the evidence of being unequally yoked, it still seemed hard for me to break free from this person. I thought, "What if he gets saved?" This was a lie of the devil. Up to that point in my life, I had never had a problem telling any man "Good-bye." Yet it was hard with him. He asked me to come back and bought my plane ticket again. I went back a second time. That was my last time. When I arrived, he was calmer since I already knew about his occultic practices. However, even odder things happened on this visit. One night while we were watching a show about home improvement on the TV in his living room, he switched the channel to a show about witchcraft. He said, "You wouldn't know anything about that." I replied, "You are right. I don't." Then he told me that werewolves were real, and I told him that I didn't believe that. He looked at me with confusion on his face and said,

"Okay." That was my last visit to his place. At the time, there were a few people attending the church I went to who were a part of Freemasonry, Sororities and/or Fraternities so I thought to myself that there might still be time for him to repent and give his life to the Lord. Fortunately, God was still talking to me. God told me He was going to get me out of this situation. The entire experience was strange; it was as if something was tampering with my free will to block me from leaving the man alone.

I finally left on a flight back to St. Louis. By this time, I felt so much shame for having gone back despite knowing the man was involved in the occult and freemasonry. Although I was not physically intimate with him, I knew that I had crossed a boundary that made it a sin. As the plane flew towards St. Louis, I was telling God, "Don't strike this plane down and kill me." The following week, I went to church; I sat all the way in the back. I still felt ashamed and dirty. I felt like others saw my sin. After the preacher finished preaching, I finally felt something break off of me. I then repented for my sin and asked God to forgive me.

After Church, I went back home and fell asleep. Around 2 AM, I saw the man I was in a relationship with walk into my room. He was in a translucent spirit-looking form. The shadowy figures of a black lion and a black lioness followed him into my bedroom. He had astral projected into my room! He walked to the side of my bed and grabbed my hand. Then he said, "You belong to me." I snatched my hand away and I said, "No, I belong to Jesus."

The next day that relationship was over. The spell was broken, and I finally saw him as he really was. That man was a warlock. He was trying to initiate me into witchcraft through rebellion. That is why the black lioness followed the black lion. Rebellion is as the sin of witchcraft. I found out later that he was in fact the devil's agent sent on assignment. The devil wanted me out of the way to get to my entire family. It is a tactic of the devil to send his agents to tempt God's people into rebellion and witchcraft. If you are prophetic, be very prayerful and discern the relationships that enter your life. Modern-day Jezebels go after the prophets. Both men and women can possess a Jezebel-like spirit. The assignment of Jezebel was to destroy God's prophets.

As I examined the patterns within my family, I learned that we had family members who were freemasons and daughters of the eastern star. The women in my immediate family did not become eastern stars. Despite that, they saw devastation from being connected to a Masonic bloodline. Here are some of things I witnessed. Most of the women in my family did not marry or stay married. If they did not marry a mason, the marriage would not last long; it would end up in divorce or death. Their first husbands would eventually divorce them and/or die. For instance, my aunt's ex-husband died of a heart attack sometime after their divorce. He was around the age of 52. My mom's husband (and my father) died two weeks after a car accident. My dad died right at 40 years old. The demonic spirit of death was transferred through the covenant and soul tie of marriage. Although their relationships ended, they were not delivered from what was in my family's bloodline due to previous generations being in freemasonry.

I believe everyone needs to go through deliverance before they get married. It would save a lot of heartache and unnecessary battles. Without deliverance, things could go well for seven years and then suddenly you could find yourself fighting your spouse's demons. The demons could be demons of addiction, infidelity, poverty, occultic roots, and even witchcraft. We need to get delivered before we get married. Everyone who is waiting on God to send them a godly spouse, needs to get free from demonic oppression and influence by going through deliverance before God sends them that godly spouse.

When the women in my family remarried, they would marry freemasons. Their second marriage with freemasons would last longer but would have a lot of spiritual warfare. My cousin's father was a freemason, and her mother was an eastern star. My cousin's first marriage ended in divorce. The second marriage was to a freemason. Shortly after that marriage, her health declined and she later died. Another family member married a freemason and shortly afterwards, her life went into chaos: her pregnant daughter and one-year old grandchild were tragically murdered by her estranged ex-husband.

As I examined my life, I realized that I also attracted men who I would later find out were freemasons. If they did not approach me themselves, someone would try to hook me up with one. Wherever I was employed, the eastern stars would attempt to hook me up with their nephews who were freemasons. One tried to hook me up with her nephew by telling me all the good qualities about him. When she showed me a picture of him, he was dressed in ancient Egyptian attire with a mic in his hand, talking to a large crowd of people. Yes, he was attractive. After looking at that picture, I was getting all kind of downloads from God about the importance of staying away from that man. I asked her, "Is he a mason?" She said, "yes." I said, "he looks angry in that picture." She smirked. I told her, "No, thank you." I wanted no part of that. I knew it was demonic and came with generational curses. God used those experiences to wake me up. After the Lord showed me that I was in a spiritual war, I could never go back to being ignorant. I learned deeper reasons for why things happened.

Chapter Three

The War with the Gates of Hell Begins

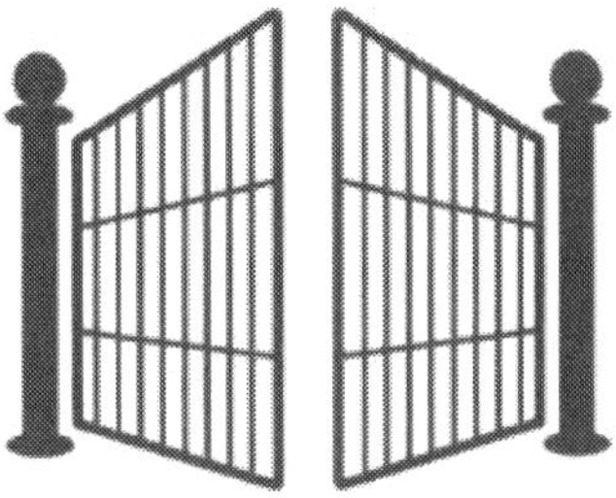

It was my birthday, about a year before I met the man from Seattle through online dating. I was right around the corner from 40 years old. I was getting "old". My friend called, asking: "What do you want to do for your birthday?" At this point, I was tired of the same thing again and again. However, I didn't have any idea of what else to do. Well, let's go out to eat, I thought. Let me tell the girls that I would like to go to Brio's. The food was good last time. As I got ready, I looked in the mirror and I wondered, "Where has all of the time gone?" I thought I would have accomplished so much by now. I could not help but think that nothing had fallen into place the way I had hoped and thought it would. My whole life, I had laid down for others. Was this what God wanted me to do? Why was I not married yet? What was wrong with me? Why do freemasons keep approaching me? Every man that has approached me, when I have asked you Lord, your answer is "No." Lord, you told me at 23 years old when I walked away from my boyfriend that he was not my husband. I had been obedient throughout the years and was now left wondering where the husband the Lord had for me was?

For all my twenties and well into my thirties, I had been "on call" for others. At a moment's notice, whenever someone needed me for something. I would go running. I thought I was serving the Lord. However, now I wondered, "Have I just been going around and around in circles like the Israelites in the wilderness?" I dismissed the barrage of thoughts and moved on. I did not have time to wait on God for the answer right now. It is always worth it to wait on God. If you were to wait on God for ten years for the answer to a question, the wait was always worth what might have seemed to be your eternity. However, if you do not wait on God, but try to "help" Him bring forth your answer, you will be busy doing nothing. Nothing of eternal value or lasting worth. Busyness without kingdom purpose is a waste of time.

As I looked at the clothes in my closet, I chose a nice shirt and some jeans. I decided I would wear this. I did not have time to think about my life right then. I did not want to be late and have them waiting for me. As I drove to the restaurant, I couldn't stop thinking about what I felt was wrong with my life. I finally decided it would be far better to think about the positive things in my life. For instance, I discovered my gift in teaching. I was working at a good corporate job. I was also teaching in children's ministry. I also had a side job teaching Excel to IT students. I was doing my best to use the gift of teaching that God had given me. Why did I still feel like there should be more? Eventually, I realized that the major problem was "I." There were too many "I s" in what I was thinking. There are many people walking in the giftings of the Spirit and the callings of God but not walking in God's Plan for their life. They only stay in the shallow waters and never move on to the deeper things of God.

Then, I remembered someone approaching me from that IT class to see if I had wanted to go on a date. God said, "NO". He was a freemason. Why do those men involved with the freemasons keep approaching me? I want no part of it. I hate that freemasonry was on my bloodline. Why did my great-grandfather have to join? Look at the women in my family, it has been a mess. Jesus, I would rather it be just You and me than to be yoked with another accursed thing.

I finally made it to Brio's. I walked in and saw the ladies I was meeting sitting down. That is so sweet, I thought, they even have balloons on the chair. The girls said in unison, "Happy Birthday!" I love them, I thought. They came out to celebrate with me. We all hugged each other and then I sat down. I am going to order the usual I thought. The waitress approached the table, "What would you like to drink?" I said, "I already know what I want. I would like a lemonade and the salmon dish." The waitress says, "Okay. Got it."

We all catch up. I am not even paying attention to the time. The waitress comes back with my order. "This looks good," I declared as I started to take a bite. Then, my phone rang. "Oh, it is my sister. I will call her back," I said as I let it go to voicemail. Then, it rang again.

This time I answered, asking: "Is everything ok?" She responds, "No, it is Isaiah." I asked, "What is wrong with Isaiah?" Roz replied, "It is like some demon got a hold of him and he is talking crazy. He is saying he wants to kill himself."

Isaiah was only nine years old. He is too young to be talking like that. My friends asked, "Is everything okay?" I replied, "No, I have to leave to check on my nephew." One of my friends said, "I will come with you."

When we arrived at my sister's town home, I could sense a strong demonic presence the very moment we walked through the door. My niece was on the phone, asking her other aunt for help. My sister looked distressed. I asked her, "What happened?" She said that Isaiah was drawing suicidal pictures of himself. Her daughter, Rae, showed her the pictures and then he started manifesting. She told me that she put on worship music and Isaiah then announced, "I am one of Satan's strongest soldiers named king. I am the second-in- command."

My friend and I immediately began to pray in the spirit; I did not know what else to do. While we were praying, my friend saw a vision of a contract. My nephew then said, "it is too strong for me; I cannot control it anymore. I see the demon standing right there." We continued to pray for hours. Then, I finally felt a release to leave. The demons, however, were not cast out; they only went dormant for a couple of years.

After we left my sister's place, it dropped into my spirit that Isaiah was dealing with thousands of demons. After this, we looked for help for him. One lady that did deliverance found it "hard to believe that a child his age would have thousands of demons." That lady would not take the case. The friend that came with me to my sister's that night even began to think he may have just been "acting out". That was far from the truth. As you continue with me, you will discover how my nephew became demonized with so many demons.

During the couple of years while the demons were dormant, I was busy and distracted; Satan's two strongest strategies are to keep us busy and distracted. I was distracted by trips, the man from Seattle, busyness at the church, work, hours on the phone with friends, and many other unfruitful activities. Finally, it was time to back out of the wilderness of distractions. However, while in the wilderness God told me to move to Texas. The moment I decided to obey him by moving, there was resistance to the move. However, I finally packed up and moved away from my friends and family.

My family depended on me to fight their spiritual battles. While they were "living their best life", I was busy interceding for their souls for years. I was a spiritual crutch for my family, their go-to for prayer, healing, and deliverance. Deliverance and salvation go hand and hand. GOD used the spiritual battles to get their attention. However, it was draining me spiritually. I am not their savior; Jesus is their savior. When I finally moved to Texas, my personal prayer life increased. A lot of distractions were out of the way. I began to strongly intercede for the salvation of my family. Despite interceding for my family, I knew that it was their choice to choose GOD. GOD gives everyone freewill and we cannot make anyone surrender to Jesus. It must be their choice.

Eventually my sister called me, saying: "I am moving to Texas because my lease is up." I said, "Okay." I had been enjoying my undistracted alone time with God for about two years by this time. However, the day my sister was supposed to move, our cousin didn't show up to drive the truck. He could not be reached anywhere. Apparently, the enemy did not want her to move near me or even just away from the principality ruling over St. Louis. I began to intercede on her behalf, and God provided a stranger to help her by driving the truck for 10 hours straight! She had to trust him to drive the U-Haul truck with all her stuff in it. When she and her children arrived in Texas, their apartment was not ready by their move-in date. My sister and her four kids had no other options. There was no way I was going to let my sister and her four kids end up on the streets. My "yes" to them moving in with me in the meantime caused

"World War III" to break out in my apartment. I went through months of spiritual warfare for the soul of my now 11-year-old nephew, Isaiah.

About 10 years prior to all of this, God had told me to stop praying for my sister. She had given her life to the LORD but was going in and out of relationship with God. It broke my heart. When I looked at her, I discerned that the enemy had her mind. While in tears, I got down on my knees and prayed, "LORD, save my sister. Have mercy on her and bring her back to you." The LORD said, "Get up! Stop praying for her." I asked the LORD, "Why?" He told me, "She chose to walk away. It is going to be a while for her to come back. She is going to have to go through a lot before she comes back to me."

God needed me to stop praying for her because He knew better than I did what my sister needed. I was obedient and got out of God's way. The Bible tells us that once the prodigal has had enough, he comes to himself (Luke 15:11-32). For those who need this for their own family, go back and read the account of the prodigal son. Where were his father and brother when he was eating in the pig pen? The prodigal son had to come to himself on his own and receive the chastening of Lord before he came back home.

The next few weeks were about a head-on collision with the kingdom of darkness and its forces of evil. The battle of good versus evil had landed on my doorstep.

Chapter Four

DEALING WITH THE FAMILY GATE

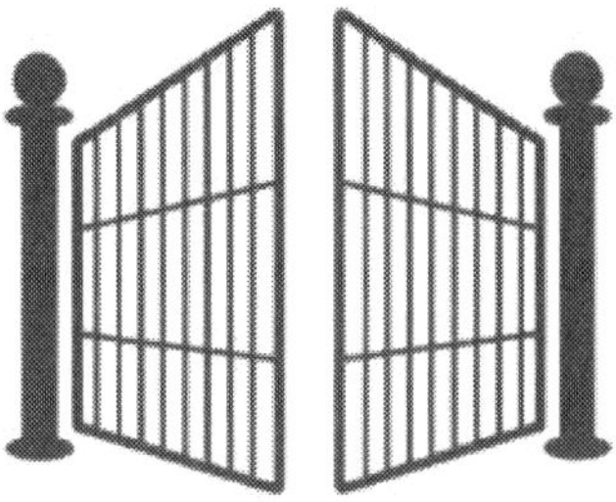

When my sister, Roz, asked, "Can we stay with you until my apartment is ready?" I said, "Yes." I knew this yes was coming with a battle, but I did not yet know what that involved. When they came to my door, I immediately recognized that all of them were demonized. As they approached the door, they looked at me with glazed looks in their eyes. I asked, "Melo, what is wrong?" Melo cried profusely while covering his eyes with his hands. Melo wouldn't even look at me. Roz picked him up and brought him inside. He was not talking and was showing signs of what doctors would diagnose as autism. Please do not misunderstand, I am not demonizing autism but there has been a dramatic rise in diagnoses of it over the years. Do you think this is by chance? I believe there is something spiritual and scientific that is going on behind the scenes concerning autism as well as many other mental health challenges.

I looked at my niece Rae (19 years old), my nephew Isaiah (11 years old), my nephew Elijah (9 years old), and my nephew Melo (2 years old). They had all grown up so much since I last saw them. I had been in the middle of worship before they knocked on the door. During my worship time, I was working while also playing worship music.

My nephew Isaiah immediately started manifesting when he entered my place. The demon spoke out of him, saying boldly: "I don't want to hear that." I knew that it was not him that was speaking, but rather it was a demon speaking through Isaiah. I decided to keep doing what I had been doing. They had not even been in my place for 5 minutes yet. Isaiah then broke out in fits of rage against his mother. I immediately started praying in the spirit. I let her handle her son. This went on for hours until I was done working.

When it was time for me to get off work, I started to look for places or people who do deliverance. I knew I was going to need help with him based on my prior experience with Isaiah years before. It was those same demons, but this time they were stronger and there were apparently more of them. My nephew was no longer there. He was no longer simply oppressed but now seemed to be fully possessed. While I was working, my sister was also there working from home. However, she couldn't really work at all. He would physically unplug her computer and could also somehow supernaturally cause her computer to have issues. The demon started controlling the technology supernaturally and let us know he was doing it. I prayed within my spirit much of that time. I would not let those evil spirits rule my house. I was getting close to putting him and his mother out. However, I knew Jesus wanted to use me to help her.

This time, my sister was sincere about giving her life back to Jesus. After the devil had beat her up so badly, she finally came to herself. Remember, God had told me about 10 years earlier that she was going to have to go through a lot before she came back to Him.

The demonic activity was so great that I would have to physically wrestle Isaiah and pray in the spirit at the same time. If I did not physically restrain him, he would try to fight everyone. He was trying to stop me from playing worship music because the demons could not stand to hear it. It almost seemed that all we had to do was breathe and the demons wanted to fight us. While wrestling him and praying, I was commanding the demonic spirits to come out of him in the name of Jesus. They were becoming even more resistant. On the first day they were in my place, I wrestled with him for over 12 hours until almost daybreak. Fortunately, God gave me supernatural strength because that demon was strong. The demonic spirit eventually spoke out, saying: "You are strong." It was only the Lord Jesus Christ that kept me going during the fight that first day by the power of the Holy Spirit.

"Finally, my brethren, be strong in the Lord, and in the power of his might. Put on the whole armor of God, that ye may be able to stand against the wiles of the devil. For we wrestle not against flesh and blood, but against principalities, against powers, against the rulers of the darkness of this world, against spiritual wickedness in high *places*." (Ephesians 6:10-13, KJV)

After the 12 hours of trying to restrain my nephew, I was saturated in sweat yet still praying. It looked like I had jumped into the shower with all my clothes still on. Then, the demonic spirit spoke out of my 11-year-old nephew: "I am dying, you are killing me." I yelled out, "I am not giving up. Die in this body and come out of my nephew." Then the demon said, "Satan, help me." To which I said, "Satan is not coming." The demon was weak. He wasn't putting up a fight and was almost limp. Then, I heard the demonic spirit say, "Satan is here." Immediately, I discerned a very dark presence. The atmosphere totally changed in my apartment and the demons started to regain their strength.

At that moment, all I could do was call on the name of Jesus. I said, "Lord Jesus, I don't think I can go any longer. This demon is not coming out." I believe at that very moment, God sent an army of angels. I remembered I conversation that I had with a friend. She had shared while we were praying and talking, "I see God sending you an army of angels. They are in full battle armor." I received it. However, At the time, I remember I thought to myself, "Why do I need an army of angels?" I clearly did not fully understand that vision at the time when she told me about it. The Lord Jesus was sending help because I was battling the very gates of hell for the souls of my nephew and family. I believe this one battle was connected to millions of souls.

Once the demon regained strength, he stopped wrestling me and just sat there. I believe God made him sit down so that I could rest. I had only a couple of hours left before I needed to get to sleep for work tomorrow. I was really concerned. My nephew was completely possessed. I had to trust God to protect us while we slept, because the demons in my nephew kept him up at night. He just stayed on the couch and stared straight forward.

Every morning at 5 AM, I would wake up to pray throughout the whole house. Before my family moved in with me, I would do this often. The morning after wrestling with my nephew, as I was walking through the house praying, Isaiah was still on the couch, wide awake. He apparently did not sleep that night. As I was walking and praying in the spirit, my nephew's eyes followed me from the couch. However, it wasn't my nephew's eyes. My nephew's eyes were brown. The eyes that stared at and followed my every move were black and possessed by darkness. (Matthew 6:23)

Once I finished praying, the demon mockingly said, "Amen. You missed a spot." I ignored him. I got myself together and logged into my computer for work. My sister also woke up and logged into her computer for work. Somehow, God gave me supernatural strength to work. I was still seeking revelation from the Lord concerning where to turn for help. I moved here relatively recently. I didn't really know anyone yet. The church I attended at that time was not that kind of church. I had never seen them do deliverance on anyone. As I began looking for help, I thought to myself, "I never heard of a demon calling on Satan. What was Isaiah into?" Lord Jesus, help me. Again, I was ready for my sister to move out. However, I knew if she left now something horrible would most likely happen to her and the children.

The demon spoke out of my nephew, confirming my concerns by stating: "I am going to kill you all." I calmly said, "Devil, you can't take my life without Jesus' permission. Right now, I am covered under the blood of Jesus." At that point, I was ready to fight a demonic army for my nephew's soul. Then, the demon spoke out of him again, "I am taking him to hell." I replied, "You are not taking him to hell. Come out of him, in the name of Jesus." I did not want to talk to the demon, but my nephew's soul was apparently not in his body.

When you stop to think about it, Christians talk to demonized people every day. When someone says they want to kill or harm themselves, what spirit do you think is speaking out of them? When someone works at a mental institution, who are those workers speaking too? Unfortunately, the truth is that they are speaking to demonic spirits in these instances. Please, ask the Lord for the gift of the discerning of spirits. Keep in mind that everyone that is angry or lying does not always have a demon. Some sins and behaviors come from the lust of our own flesh. However, some sins come from demonic influence.

Now, I was once again wrestling with my nephew. It was very physical. My sister was not saved but was doing her best to hold him down. At times, however, she would get in her flesh and that would serve to feed those demons and empower them. The dust is the food of the serpent (Genesis 3:14). Our flesh is that dust. It was extremely difficult to do deliverance on him because the demonic entities kept being strengthened and empowered in this way. While I was praying in the spirit, she was operating in the flesh. We had no help but the Holy Spirit.

There were also legal rights that kept my nephew from freedom. The following are some examples of legal rights: a person's will, generational curses or iniquities, sins, rebellion, disobedience and unforgiveness. Some people have made demons their "pets" and enjoy the sins the demons push them to do. However, the demons are never satisfied until they completely ruin the person's life. The body is a person's temple and that temple houses their soul, their spirit, and the Holy Spirit or demonic spirits. The demons want the person's temple condemned and unusable. If a house is condemned, the house needs to be torn down. When the human body is destroyed, their spirit goes to heaven or hell. The demons want to take as many souls as they can to hell to be with them there for eternity.

At this point, I needed to phone a friend. I didn't want to wrestle these demons in my nephew every day. I needed a breakthrough in delivering my nephew from these demonic oppressors. I reached out to a friend and told her what was going on. My friend and her husband prayed for me. Afterwards, I went to sleep and trusted God to protect all of us.

Chapter Five

BREAKING THROUGH THE GATE OF COMFORT

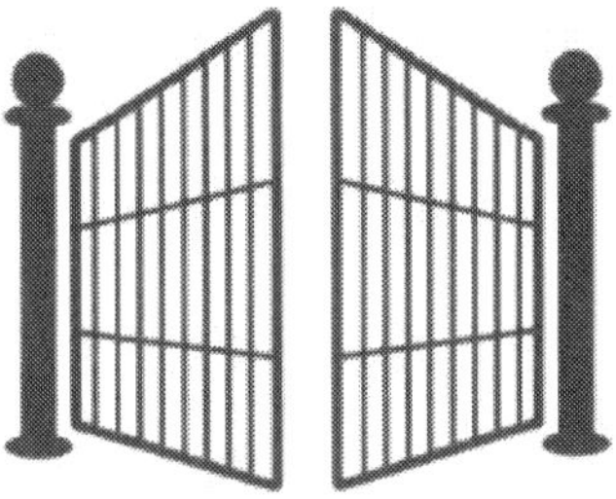

For the first time in a long while, my family went to church. They wanted to go to the church I was attending at the time. We walked right in, sat down, listened until the end, and then walked right out the church doors. This church was known for deliverance. This church preached the Word but there was no real demonstration of the Word. It made me wonder what are we doing with the Word? Not one church member, walked up to us to ask, "Do you need prayer?" My possessed nephew just sat there; no one acknowledged him. My nephew was comfortable going there. How many people are walking into church with demons and then leaving with the same demons? It is time to break out of our comfort zone and begin to walk in a true relationship with the Lord Jesus Christ.

Someone once told me the main principality ruling over America is comfort. We are so comfortable that demons are even comfortable attending our church services. We are so comfortable that witches and warlocks can join the church and still practice witchcraft. They can get on the intercessory team and even get in some pulpits. These people are not being convicted of changing their ways by the Holy Spirit but instead are changing the atmosphere of the church. Why? The Word is not being preached with its power being demonstrated and witchcraft is not being rebuked.

I met some witches that went to Church and were extremely friendly. I discerned that they were witches. The Holy Spirit led me to have evidence of this, and these are not false accusations. The purpose He revealed it to me was to warn and protect God's people. Without real discernment, some true believers would say that those witches and warlocks were "good Christians". However, they are "tares" who are willing to do the unfruitful "busy work" of the ministry. Witches can get saved, but God's people should still rightly discern the spirits people carry. Jesus died for them to come out of witchcraft, not for us to stay buddies with them.

When the Holy Bible refers to comfort, the Hebrew meaning of the root word is to call to one's side, call for, summon, address, encourage, strengthen by consolation, and to teach. When we look at the secular definition of comfort, it is a state of physical ease, freedom from pain or anxiety, or the act of soothing and providing consolation. God did not call us to live a life of ease and freedom from all pain. We all must instead bear our cross (Luke 9:23), and carrying a cross comes with some form of pain and uneasiness. This situation with my nephew and family was pulling me out of my comfort zone and into my calling. However, I did not see this until later.

CHAPTER SIX

BREAKING THROUGH THE GATE OF COMFORT – PART 2

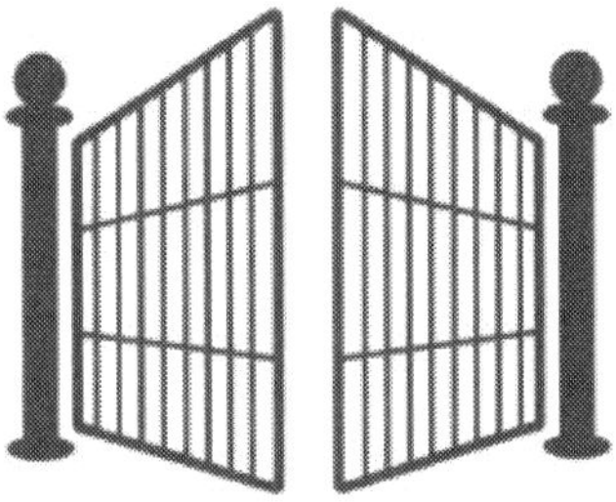

I continued to pray. Prayer is so important. I would not have made it without prayer. My sister's apartment was still not ready. I believed it was being supernaturally held up for a reason. At this point, I was praying that my sister and her children would all surrender their lives to the Lord Jesus. I was constantly playing worship music. It still irritated the demons within my nephew. No one had responded to my emails for help with his deliverance. During this time, I was also emailing all sorts of various ministries to ask for help and no one responded. I do not normally ask for help. I was so used to getting stuff done on my own. God humbled me during this challenging season; we all need the help of our brothers and sisters in Christ. We are the "Body of Christ", his Bride. The arm needs hands. Any body part that is disconnected will begin to die. What amazed me was that I didn't even get one reply; no one even wrote to say, "we cannot help you."

I found out later just how deep my nephew was into the occult. I don't blame them for not responding. Who wants unnecessary and/or unapproved warfare? "And David enquired at the LORD, saying, Shall I pursue after this troop? Shall I overtake them? And he answered him, Pursue: for thou shalt surely overtake *them*, and without fail recover *all*." (1 Samuel 30:8, KJV) It is entirely possible that God told them not to help me. God wanted all the glory. The good news was that I had Jesus and the host of the Lord's army helping me.

I would still talk to my nephew about Jesus with no response from him. The movie "Come out in Jesus' name" was playing at the theaters. I heard about people being delivered at the movie theater while watching "Come Out in Jesus Name." I talked to my sister and suggested that we go to see it. We rode in the car with my fully demonized nephew and trusted God to protect us. On the way to the movie, those demons started speaking out of my nephew. The evil spirits laughed as they taunted us, saying: "Watch what is going to happen."

While we were sitting in the theatre, the scene suddenly went black, right before the deliverance part. No deliverance took place. Then, the demons began to laugh sinisterly. The demons somehow knew that the deliverance part was being cut out before we went into the theaters. We left the theater and went back home, very discouraged.

Every night, I slept very lightly. When I slept, the Lord would wake me up the moment my nephew was on the way towards my bedroom door. He would come and just stare at me. He would say, "Oh, you are awake." Then, he would turn around and go back to the couch. I would then fall back to sleep. I was still in the middle of the war; sleep was a privilege at that time.

Chapter Seven

The Eye and Ear Gates

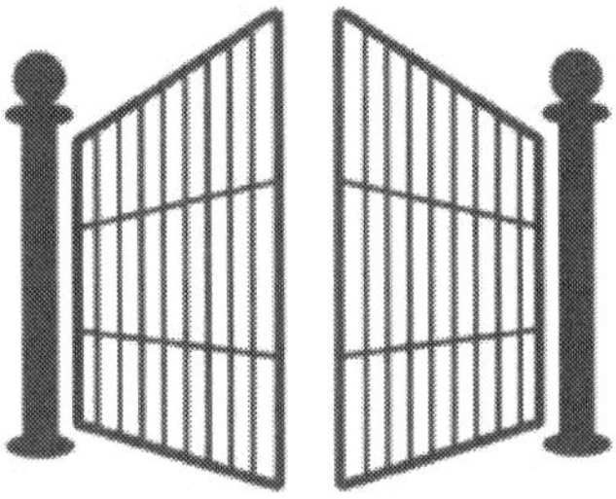

I woke up far earlier than daybreak. It must still be in the middle of the night, I thought. I started praying, and as I looked up, I could see Isaiah standing at my bedroom door, staring at me once again. As I looked into his eyes, it was not my nephew staring back at me. The demon spoke, "You sleep light." Then, he went back to the living room. I didn't want to talk to those spirits at all, but my nephew was fully possessed. People unknowingly talk with demons every day. What do you think is talking when another person curses you out? We are not wrestling against flesh and blood (Ephesians 6:12). What about that person that lied to you? Sometimes those are evil spirits influencing people to do and to say certain things. (Gen 19:1-26)

I didn't have a moment of fear and didn't allow anger to rise in me. I only wanted those demons to pay for what they did to my family.

I wanted those demons out of my nephew. I felt compassion for my nephew, and I knew that it was not him that was doing or saying all these things. I knew there were some deep things going on because he was **fully** possessed. My nephew had no apparent control over his body.

The devil wanted to take me out. Nevertheless, I knew Jesus is my strong tower. I had experience with the Lord protecting me from danger. "For he shall give his angels charge over thee, to keep thee in all thy ways." (Ps 91:11) My faith in his protection was increased. I flashed back to a time when I was going to college. At the time, I worked in the day and went to college at night. When I went to class one night, as I drove into the parking lot, I noticed an unusual number of cars on the lot. There were no parking spaces that were close to the building. The closest spot was really far away from the door.

After class, the professor dismissed us. By this time, it was very dark outside. It was about 9:30 PM. At this time in my life, I had a bad habit of waiting to get my keys out until I got close to my car. The voice in my spirit said, "Get your keys ready; do not speak to them. Just get in the car and drive." When I heard that, I had no fear. I simply obeyed. I got my keys ready in my hand before I even left the building. As I walked out of the building, I saw almost no cars left in the parking lot. I looked and saw my car far away. Next to my car, there was a car with very dark tinted windows and the engine running. This was strange because our cars were the only two left in the parking lot. It was far away from the building. I chose to walk normally to the car. As I got closer, I noticed that there were at least two men in the car. The man on the passenger side had his window down. I kept walking towards my car until I got right next to the door of my car. The man in the car next to me said, "How are you doing?" I said nothing and opened my door really fast. I was out of the parking lot before he could even finish talking. It was like God froze time; it was like they were frozen in their car until I got into my car safely.

When I went back to my Spanish class the next week, the teacher informed us that someone was robbed on the same day as our class last week. She told all of us to be careful. I lived in a dangerous city. That city made the list for most murders in the United States. I learned to trust God to protect me and knew if God protected me then, he would surely do it now.

I was not giving up on my nephew. I would fight the gates of hell for his soul if I knew God was with me. Jesus already won the war! It was during this warfare for my nephew that the Holy Spirit revealed to me that demons feed off flesh, especially when we are operating in our flesh. "And the LORD God said unto the serpent, because thou hast done this, thou *art* cursed above all cattle, and above every beast of the field; upon thy belly shalt thou go, and the dust shalt thou eat all the days of thy life" (Genesis 3:14). The dust referred to in that scripture represents the flesh. Our flesh came from the dust of the earth, and the kingdom of darkness draws strength when we are operating in the flesh. The flesh is the sin nature man operates in before becoming sanctified and set apart for the Lord.

While my sister and I were working, the demonic spirit would constantly manifest through Isaiah. It was very hostile and full of rage. At the time, I didn't have much experience in deliverance. I believed the Word of God and that I had the power to cast out devils in Jesus' name. However, prior to this situation, I had only done deliverance twice on family members. One of my family members had been in her room and then came to me for help. She said she felt like the walls were caving in on her and that she was losing her mind. Jesus used me to command that evil spirit to come out of her, to release her. She screamed with a loud voice and never had another problem like that again.

I believed God could use me, but there was something much deeper going on here. I had been commanding those evil spirits to leave in the name of Jesus for hours and for many days. Yet, nothing had happened. When I asked the spirit to tell its name, it told me some ancient name that I couldn't even pronounce. I thought that demons were named based upon their character (or the way in which they functioned against the person hosting them) like anger or rage. Later, I received greater revelation on where demons came from. Demons once walked the earth and had actual names.

Once again, I asked Jesus to help me. Then, the evil spirit said, "I am from the marine kingdom." It stopped suddenly and said, "I told you too much." At that time, I didn't know what the marine kingdom was. When I pondered what it could mean, the Disney movie the "Little Mermaid" came to mind. Disney is very occultic and even has some of the Church deceived into thinking it is harmless. The Little Mermaid is about the marine kingdom. The demonic marine kingdom is associated with witchcraft, perversion, and the occult. All Disney's cartoons have some form of witchcraft in them. Have you ever noticed there is always a wicked witch, fairy godmother, or a good witch somewhere within the storyline? However, up until now I didn't really know anything about that. God said his people perish for a lack of knowledge (Hosea 4:6).

To think, people are blindly going to church and still have no idea about spiritual warfare.

I even visited a well-known mega church that promoted that movie and gave out free tickets. The minister said, "She was a holy mermaid." Mermaids are demonic beings. In biblical times, the Philistines worshipped Dagon, a demonic prince of the abyss. To celebrate and watch that movie blindly, is to give the demonic kingdom worship by giving your attention to it. Just by watching those movies, you give the devil access to your eye and ear gates. Some demonic spirits can come through watching demonic stuff. No matter what, you are taking in things from the kingdom of darkness, and that creates a mixture and God hates that.

When I heard the demonic spirit possessing my nephew state that it was from the marine kingdom, I declared, "you evil marine spirit, get out in Jesus' name." The evil spirit said that only God could cast it out. I didn't understand. That evil spirit called himself, Satan's number one soldier. The Holy Spirit revealed to me that Leviathan was one of the evil spirits speaking out of Isaiah. Later, I read in the bible about Leviathan. Isaiah 27:1 states: "In that day the LORD with his sore and great and strong sword shall punish leviathan the piercing serpent, even leviathan that crooked serpent; and he shall slay the dragon that *is* in the sea." According to the scripture, God must deal with Leviathan. The sea is the marine kingdom.

The Bible tells us that Leviathan is a king over all the children of pride (Job 41:34). My nephew was full of pride. Even at his young age, he was very prideful. It went for years, going unchecked because of the state of his mother. After he informed me that, "Only God can cast me out", Isaiah lay down on the couch with his legs crossed. I had to make sure that I stayed out of the flesh. The Holy Spirit somehow kept me from snatching that boy up and grabbing a belt. I had to remember that I was dealing with an evil spirit and not simply my nephew. The Word of God says that "foolishness *is* bound in the heart of a child; *But* the rod of correction shall drive it far from him (Proverbs 22:15, KJV). However, this was not just a child I was talking to, this was an ancient evil spirit. The demons were operating out of a child's body.

Chapter Eight

Who Are the Demonic Gatekeepers?

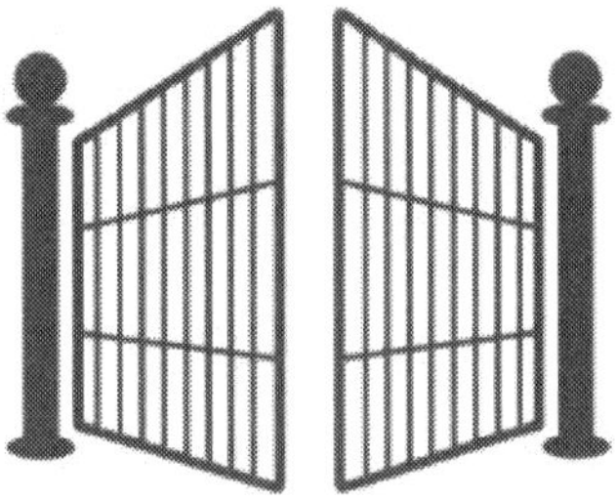

I woke up and logged in for work. I had my nephew sit next to me. His mom had bought them all a Bible. I thought, I must get the Word of God into him. While sitting at my desk beside my nephew, I had flashback memories. The first memory was of when he was around the age of 3 years old and I had mentioned the name of Jesus. He said, "Jesus," and I asked, "What do you know about Jesus?" My nephew replied, "I know my Jesus." I looked at him amazed. The second memory was from when his mom started to go back to Church. I had stopped by her place and there was a woman sitting at her kitchen table. When I walked in, I felt a reaction to the woman in the pit of my stomach. The woman looked at me and said, "Hi." I replied, "Hi." Next thing I knew,

I heard God say to stay away from her. So, when she asked me, "Do you want to hang out with us?" I simply said, "No." She said, "We can do something without any men or alcohol." I said, "No, thanks." I thought to myself, "What is my sister doing hanging out with her?" Later on, I warned my sister about her. However, my sister ignored my warning. Slowly, my sister began to drift away from the Lord again. After this my sister left the Church. That woman was a witch - she practiced with tarot cards. This whole experience broke my heart all over again. After all of the fasting and praying for my sister's salvation, she walked away from God again.

My sister's decisions clearly affected her children also. Now look at the state of her children. This time my nephew was calm while he sat next to me at my workstation. I looked down at his NIV Bible and noticed he had certain words underlined in Genesis 6. I remembered some of the words: **Nephilim, thoughts only evil**, and **regret**. After looking down at his bible, I stated: "You are not my nephew." He said, "You are right." Then, that evil spirit began to act out again, violently. This went on for over 10 hours; it went on for so long that I lost track of time.

I believe that demons are disembodied Nephilim spirits. The story of how the Nephilim were created is found in Genesis 6:2 where the Bible tells us, "That the sons of God saw the daughters of men, that they *were* beautiful; and they took wives for themselves of all whom they chose." The Bible continues to tell us how there were giants on earth in those days and also afterwards due to the intermingling of the seed of the sons of God and the daughters of men (Genesis 6:4). This intermingling led to great perversion and wickedness over all the earth, and the very heart of the Lord was grieved, leading Him to decide to destroy the corrupted bloodline through the great flood. However, despite the flood, the Nephilim somehow survived and the presence of giants was reported by the scouts sent into the promised land when they reported back to Joshua (Numbers 13:32-33).

Others believe that the angels which chose to follow Lucifer when he was expelled from Heaven later became demons. However, I believe fallen angels are different from demons. Although angels have celestial bodies, they can also take on the actual physical form of a man. If the angels of the Lord can take on a human form, so could the fallen ones. The major difference between fallen angels and the Nephilim is that the spirits of the Nephilim once inhabited a body that was partly human. Their actual lineage was half from the sons of God and the other half from the daughters of men. The actual word "De-mon" is a compound word. "De" meaning from and "Mon" meaning man in old English. This points to why demons fight so hard to stay in the bodies they inhabit. Demons can only experience pleasure and pain while in physical bodies.

The Bible tells us that in the days of Noah, the men stood back and willingly let their daughters marry the sons of God who were not human. Those marriages formed covenants and agreements that gave demonic spirits the legal right to enter men. Because of this corruption of the bloodline, great evil was going on everywhere. "And GOD saw that the wickedness of man *was* great in the earth, and *that* every imagination of the thoughts of his heart *was* only evil continually." (Genesis 6:5, KJV) The hybrids which came forth through these marriages were unredeemable; they only thought evil thoughts. This explains why when people are demonized, they have evil thoughts continuously.

You may wonder what happened to the Nephilim when the earth was flooded? One explanation is that although their bodies perished, their spirits remained and the devil recruited them for the kingdom of darkness, just like the third of the angels that fell from heaven with Lucifer. One might also wonder, what happened to fallen angels that slept with the women? The Bible tells us God locked them up in chains (2 Peter 2:4 and Jude 1:6) because they had crossed boundaries and gone too far. Even Satan knows not to cross certain boundaries, that is why he came to God first before he attacked Job. Instead of crossing certain boundaries, Satan uses his powers of influence and lying persuasion.

Before the demons achieved legal access to man, Satan was only able to use persuasive lies. Eve was in full control when she committed the first sin by eating from the tree of the knowledge of good and evil. However, Satan tricked her by the power of persuasive lies. The Bible specifically warns us that enmity exists between us and Satan as a continuing consequence from when our relationship with God was broken through our disobedience when we chose to believe the persuasive deception of the serpent rather than trusting the warning God had given us concerning what the result would be of eating from the fruit of the tree of the knowledge of good and evil in Genesis 3:15, "and I will put enmity between thee (the serpent) and the woman, and between thy seed and her seed; it shall bruise thy head, and thou shalt bruise his heel." (Genesis 3:15)

The use of "enmity" points to a continual state of hatred and animosity between men and Satan. Before Cain killed Abel, the Lord asked him, "Why are you angry? And why has your countenance fallen? If you do well, will you not be accepted? And if you do not well, sin lies at the door. And its desire *is* for you, but you should rule over it. (Genesis 4:6-7, NKJV) It is important to know that you do not need to be possessed by a demon to sin. However, sin is the door of legal access that lets demons in. Once a demon gets in, it breaks down your will to say "no" to future sin. When the devil is given an inch, he will take you a mile down that road. It is important to ask the Holy Spirit for revelation of what sin in your life needs to be addressed and cut off.

Chapter Nine

Help Against the Gates

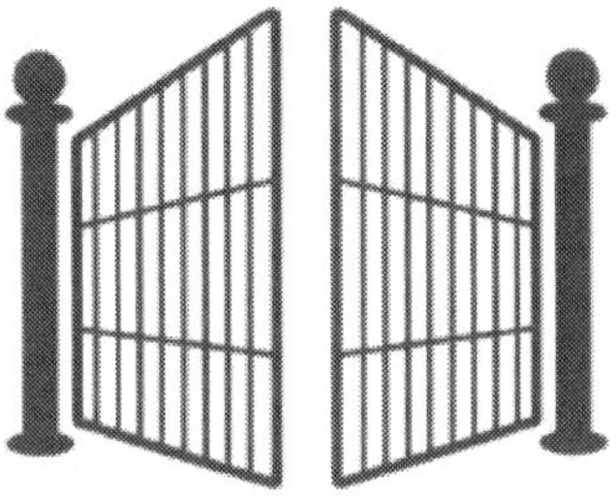

I finally received a reply to the email that I had sent out to various sources asking for prayer or help with my nephew. Although this may sound strange to you, I believe God didn't allow others to help because he wanted to do something within me. I don't believe this was just about my family. There is always a much bigger plan. "And we know that all things work together for the good to them that love God, to them who are the called according to *his* purpose." (Roman 8:28, KJV) Ask God before you immediately try to get help, even when it comes to intercession. Certain types of prayers really require extreme warfare in the spirit. If God approves, you will recover all that the enemy is trying to steal, kill, or destroy. However, if you move on your own without God's approval, you could have unnecessary warfare as well as attempts at retribution from the enemy. It was not until later that I found out how deep my nephew was into the occult. During this time, I didn't fully understand the plan that God had for my family and me.

In the email reply I received, the writer stated that he and his father did deliverance. I was desperate by this time, otherwise I would not have gone that route. We communicated via email and arranged a time for them to come to my place to help with my nephew. During those days, the evil spirits within my nephew were manifesting 24/7. This was without me even saying a word. The only relief at times was when the spirits would be spiritually bound by me "in the name of Jesus." While that spirit was bound, my nephew would sit down and just stare out into space. At other times, he would sit Indian style on the floor and stare at the wall. He would not say a word. While I was working, his mom would often have to restrain him physically.

The deliverance minister was scheduled to come after I got off work. Finally, I heard a knock at the door. I opened the door and the first thing I noticed was that the deliverance minister was young. However, I thought to myself, David took out a giant as a child (1 Samuel 17:33). He told me that his father could not make it. The LORD told me, "He is not equipped to handle this." However, I thought to myself, "Well, he is here now."

I invited him in. My nephew was sitting on the couch. I told the minister, "He is the one I emailed you about." My nephew looked at him and didn't say a word. I simply said, "We know you are in there." Suddenly, he manifested rage and put his middle finger up at us. Then he started using profanity and was very violent. God gave me supernatural strength and wrestling moves that I had never done before in my life. I began to restrain him while calling on the name of Jesus. Then, I started speaking in tongues. The deliverance minister said to the evil spirit, "Come out in the name of Jesus." The evil spirit just got angrier.

This went on for about 4-5 hours. The deliverance minister kept trying to cast the demons out without success. Hours later, I was still wrestling with my nephew, trying torestrain him. Sweat was dripping down my face and my clothes were soaked in sweat. I still had strength, but the demon spirits were getting weaker. At one point, the evil spirit said I am leaving this place. I told the evil spirits, "You are not leaving with my nephew's body."

The deliverance minister stopped to assess things. He said, "There is something deeper going on here." Personally, I felt like the deliverance minister was getting a little discouraged. He really wanted to help us. I began trying to encourage him. I told him," God has a bigger plan." Then he said, "I just came back to the Lord." I didn't want to keep him there any longer, but he didn't want to give up. Finally, I told him, "God will deliver him." I told him, "It is okay, you can go." He left. Then I told the evil spirit, "One way or another, you are getting out of my nephew's body." He asked me, "Why are you fighting so hard for him?" I did not say anything to answer his question. However, my nephew has a soul, and the Lord had told me before he was even born that he was called to be a prophet. I would not let the enemy take my nephew to hell without a fight. For now, he was staying on the couch. I went and prepared myself for bed. It had been a long day.

Chapter Ten

God's Protection Against the Gates

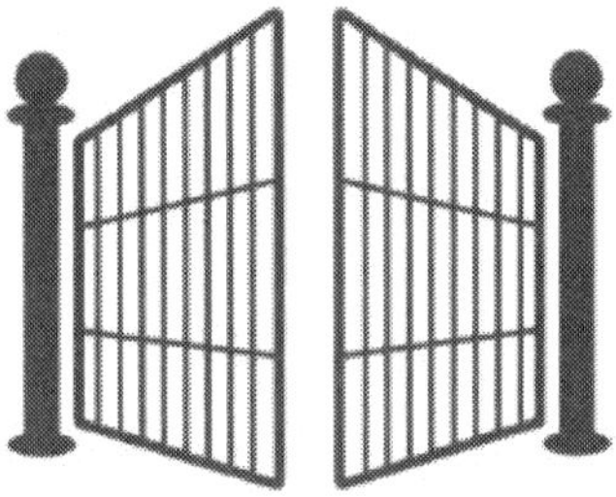

I woke up the next morning, got up and prayed. I was praying very often during this time. I was asking the Lord, what is the legal right for those evil spirits to refuse to be cast out? I understood my nephew had not given his life to the LORD yet. However, this was a whole other level of possession by the demonic spirits. After I finished praying, I logged in for work. My sister also logged in for work. My nephew never seemed to get any sleep.

My friend called and told me that after she had prayed with me, an evil spirit showed up at her place. The evil spirit had tried to retaliate against her for coming into agreement with me for my nephew's salvation. I just wanted my nephew to stay present long enough to hear the gospel, long enough for me to find out what was going on with him. The demonic spirit would no longer let my nephew's spirit interact with anyone at all. My friend who had come to pray with me was the only one I knew who was strong enough in her faith to pray with me. I did not feel that anyone else I knew was spiritually strong enough to be involved. As we were talking, I began to tell my friend about the dreams I had been having lately.

Before I could tell her anything, she said that she heard in her spirit that a woman that lived above me was a Wiccan. She had moved in after I had already been there for months. I had thought that the lady that had lived there before her was a witch as well. This was strange. I had not seen the lady living above me recently and my door camera had not picked her up. However, this would not be my first encounter with witches. I thought to myself, "What do they want with me?" At this point, I wasn't bothering anyone, nor was I a threat to anyone as I was mostly behind the scenes with my and intercession. I didn't fully understand how powerful prayers and intercession were against the powers of darkness. Now, I fully understand that kingdom of heaven suffers violence and the violent take it by force.

While I had been living in St. Louis, I had woken up one night to a translucent figure of a white man with glasses in my bedroom. He appeared to be inside of some type of translucent glass ball. I had never seen anything like that before. He was trying to break the glass, but it would just crack and then come back together. It would not break. He was angrily pounding on the glass with his fist. God let me know that he was a warlock who had astral projected into my place. He was trapped inside the glass ball. I began to pray in the spirit: "Lord, get him out of here." The next day I noticed a man that matched his description walking angrily outside my apartment in the parking lot. He didn't look at me at all. This was my first time seeing this man outside of my apartment. At that time, I had no idea about spiritual warfare or why he chose to attack me.

Spiritual warfare was never taught at the Church I attended in St. Louis. I didn't know anything about astral projection. If there were witches at that church, they were few and far between. My focus at the time was on Jesus. One night, I came home late from a church event. I parked my car in our building's lot and then I got out. As I was standing by my car, my neighbor got out of her car and started walking towards me. She was dressed from head to toe in white. She had a white wig, white dress, white stockings, and white shoes. I looked at her like, what in the world? She saw the look on my face and said while smiling, "I just came from the white and red blood cell convention. I went as a white blood cell." I said, "Okay," and went to my apartment. I did not believe her. I went into the house to look it up and did not find any kind of convention like that.

This apartment complex was in a nice St. Louis neighborhood, but the neighborhood was starting to decline. There were many things that I saw during the time that I lived there. One day I came home from work to find a flyer on my door. The flyer was from the apartment management offering free readings from the one of the top Psychics in the St. Louis/Midwest region. The twist was that to get the demonic reading, you had to donate your blood. There was no way I was doing that. God told me that my neighbor was not a fake witch but one that dealt with familiar spirits. In the Bible when King Saul of Israel no longer had the prophet Samuel to advise him, he tried to inquire of the Lord, but he heard nothing. Due to his fear of the great army of the Philistines, King Saul had his servants find him a spiritual medium and he consulted with the witch of Endor that had a familiar spirit. He wanted information without going through God and he had the witch summon the spirit of Samuel so that he could ask him what to do. Samuel chastised him for summoning him when it was clear that the Lord was no longer with Saul. Samuel continued to tell Saul that there would be dire consequences for his consulting with a medium. This act of disobedience and rebellion caused both Saul and his son, Jonathan, to lose their lives (1 Samuel 28:7-19).

Some people don't realize how dangerous it is spiritually to consult with the enemy for knowledge through psychics, mediums or other occultic practices. It is like eating from the tree of the knowledge of good and evil all over again. The moment you come into agreement with that, you don't know what the enemy is going to steal from you. When you participate in occultic practices you are granting the enemy legal access to your life and using their demonic knowledge kills destinies. Whereas God's knowledge leads you toward Jesus and His plans for your life. Well, after seeing their flyer offering access to the kingdom of darkness, I decided to make a flyer of my own and give it to the Psychic that was coming. The flyer I made said, "Jesus loves you."

After work, I went to the Leasing Office where they were having their event. The moment I got near the door of the Leasing Office, I felt a strong demonic presence. I walked in and saw people giving blood. I walked towards the Psychic and she said, "Have a seat." God told me, "Don't sit down." I simply handed her the flyer. She looked at it and chuckled. Then, I walked very fast out of there. I was so ready to get out of that atmosphere.

Approximately one week later, I was driving to work. The traffic lights turned from yellow to red. I didn't think I was going to make it through the light, and I didn't want to get a ticket. I slowed down and stopped, and the light turned red. While I was sitting at the red light, I suddenly felt the impact of a car hitting me. It pushed me hundreds of feet through the intersection and then down the street. My entire back seat and car trunk were smashed into the back of my seat. I saw a yellow school bus attached to my car. I was in shock. It was not a car that hit me, but a school bus. I realized that I could have died. I was listening to "Grace" by Tasha Cobb when the school bus hit me. I knew God spared my life and showed me grace. If someone had been in my back seat, they would have been dead.

Within minutes both the police and fire department were there. They cut me out of the car because it was so damaged that the front doors would no longer open. I was still crying as they put me on a stretcher and into the back of the ambulance. I heard the siren and heard the paramedics talking to each other about my vitals. I heard that my blood pressure was high, but it was going down. I was taken to the nearest hospital. At that moment, my adrenaline was still high, so I didn't expect to feel anything yet. They immediately took me to a hospital room. I was lying on the bed waiting for a doctor. Instead, a police officer walked in and he just sat there and stared at me for a moment. We just had a general conversation. I could tell he was trying to assess me. He told me he was just down the street when it happened. He told me, "How they build the cars now, saves lives." I said, "I thank God." He left the room.

A nurse walked in next and told me to urinate in a container. She did not tell me that they were testing me for drugs. Of course, the test came back negatively. The doctor conducted her examination. According to the doctor I appeared to be fine, no broken bones, but it was still possible I had a whiplash. All throughout these tests and the doctor's exam I was thanking Jesus for sparing my life. God certainly had his angels protecting me. "For he shall give his angels charge over thee, to keep thee in all thy ways. They shall bear thee up in *their* hands, lest thou dash thy foot against a stone" (Psalm 91:11-12, KJV). My experience taught me about God as my protector. It also prepared me for trials ahead. After the accident, God even provided me with a brand-new car!

Long before we discover our purpose or the plan of God for our lives, the enemy tries to stop us from getting there. "For I know the thoughts (devices, plans, purposes) that I think toward you, saith the LORD, thoughts of peace, and not of evil, to give you an expected (hope, expectation, outcome) end" (Jeremiah 29:11, KJV). It is not just about knowing the plan for your life, but also about knowing your purposes. In addition to knowing your purposes, it is important to know what you should be doing during each season. There are often layers of gifts and things that God has called us to. For instance, the purposes of God for your life could be to be a husband or wife, father or mother, business owner, and/or a Pastor. All these assignments are filled with purpose. "To every *thing there is* a season, and a time to every purpose under the heaven." (Ecclesiastes 3:1, KJV) Unfortunately, the enemy also has a plan to destroy our lives and we should not be ignorant of that. The enemy's plans can seem like God's plans at first glance, but at the end of it is destruction as the enemy only comes to steal, kill and destroy (John 10:10). We need to be careful "lest Satan should get an advantage of us: for we are not ignorant of his devices" (2 Cor 2:11, KJV). Some of his devices include but are not limited to mental perceptions or thoughts designed to bring forth his evil purposes.

There are two important questions to ask when there is opposition to what we are trying to accomplish. Is this going to lead me to God's purposes for my life? Is Satan trying to distract me from God's will for my life? The storm you are encountering could be leading you to right where you need to be. Remember, all things work together for the good for those that love God and are the called according to His purpose (Romans 8:28).

Chapter Eleven

Revelation of the Gates

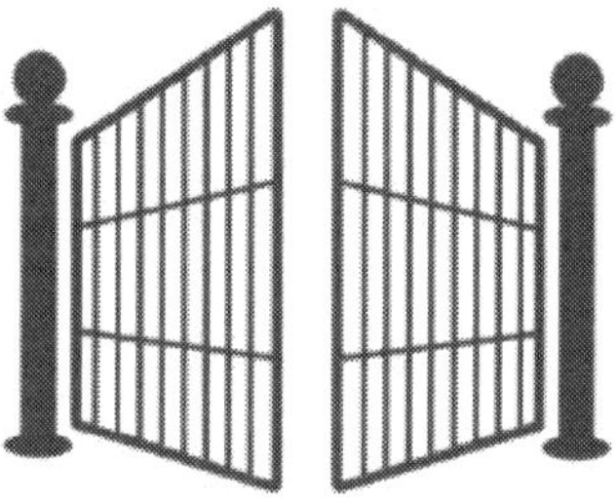

I woke up in the morning to pray before sunrise. My nephew was wide awake, sitting on the couch. Although I refer to it being my nephew, it was only his body, the evil spirits were completely controlling him. Those evil spirits watched me as I walked through my house and prayed. Why have those evil spirits not come out in Jesus' name? Did not the Word of God say that we could cast out devils? I know the Word of God is true. This whole experience was an example of why we must "study to show ourselves approved" (2 Timothy 2:15) because the bible is all about us learning how to connect the dots. "And I will give unto thee the keys of the kingdom of heaven: and whatsoever thou shalt bind on earth shall be bound in heaven: and whatsoever thou shall loose on earth shall be loosed in heaven" (Matthew 16:19, KJV). The key to understanding this is found in the scripture prior to this verse. Peter had been provided revelation knowledge that Jesus was the Son of God. Because of that revelation, that Jesus really is the Son of God, the gates of hell will not prevail against the Church. That revelation is the key that opens the door to us being able to bind and loose. I needed the Lord's revelation about what was going on with my nephew. It is not by chance that the last book of the bible is about the Revelation of Jesus Christ. Once you have a revelation of **Who** Jesus Christ really was and **Who** He wants to be in your current situation, you hold the key to the end of the battle. You still must use the key to unlock the door to your victory in Jesus Christ. Once the door is unlocked, then it is the end of that battle.

While my nephew was manifesting rage, he pulled all the plugs to the computer. I had to stop helping my sister. My sister reached out to her manager and let her know the truth; she told her manager that her son was dealing with demons. Do you think my sister's manager believed her? My sister had already missed so much time because of those demonic episodes. Her boss just told her that she could not miss any more time from work. She ended up getting fired. Now what? She could only stay with me for so long. We really needed Jesus to help us in this battle.

If my nephew wasn't physically messing with stuff directly, the demonic spirits were messing with it supernaturally. Those evil spirits had the ability to mess with technology. The evil spirits would control the television and disrupt the phone signals. If I could have physically fought them, I would have. At this point, I was so irritated that I felt like taking on the whole kingdom of darkness without fear. I'd had it with these demons. However, our weapons are not carnal. I need knowledge and wisdom from the Holy Spirit to have victory in this situation. Sometimes, it is hard to hear from the Lord when you are in the thick of a battle. I needed to remember that the battle is not ours but God's (2 Chronicles 20:15). My sister and I were now taking turns dealing with my nephew. We were constantly calling on the name of Jesus to keep the evil spirits from overpowering us.

One day my cell phone rang. I answered it. It was my close friend. She told me that, while she was at her church, a new couple was visiting that does deliverance. God must have heard my cry. I told my friend what was going on with my nephew. At that time, I didn't share this information with many people. In the past, when I had shared with some people, they either couldn't help me or would question the fact that a child could have demons. When my sister shared some things with her previous Pastor, his response didn't make it seem like he believed her. My nephew had been baptized at that Church. At the time of his baptism, our mom said she noticed something strange while watching him get baptized. My mother said "when he went down in the water, his eyes were open. He really didn't even flinch." She thought that was strange. She also noticed that he suddenly knew how to swim overnight. He was never taught how to swim. She thought that was strange. I also thought that was strange. I didn't believe that his baptism was a true transformation and repentance experience.

My friend said that she and her husband would be praying for me. Shortly after this, they met a family at her Church that did deliverance. This family had just started going to that Church. My friend said that she got their number, so she would reach out to them for help. I was immensely thankful for their intercession and help. No one should be alone in battle. God has called us to be a part of the Body of Christ. The hand is not effective without the arm; we all need each other to succeed. My friend said, "I will call you back when I hear from them." She finally called me back and said, "Lauren and her husband agreed to help." For the first time in a long time, I felt like the war could end soon.

Right after that call, my nephew started manifesting rage. He started throwing stuff. He broke some of my glass vases in the living room. My living room looked like a tornado came through it. My friend called back right when my nephew's fit of rage was happening and she called Lauren on a three-way call. While on the phone, Lauren began to start deliverance on Isaiah. My nephew was lying down on the bed at the time. She bound the demonic spirits, prohibiting them from moving. She then found out that his soul was not in his body. The demonic spirits then tried to say that we were torturing Isaiah. "We are going to take him to hell, just like we took Reese," they said. Lauren asked, "Where do you have his soul? Which kingdom?"

At this time, I did not know about spiritual kingdoms (along with most Christians). All I knew about was Heaven, Earth, and Hell. However, there are kingdoms within each realm and dimension. For instance, within the Earth there are multiple kingdoms. You have the heavens (sky), land, and oceans. On land, you have multiple continents. Within those continents, there are multiple nations. Within those nations, there are multiple ethic groups. There are also different types of waters on the earth; there are ponds, rivers, lakes, gulfs, seas, and oceans. Within the ocean, there are different levels and depths as well as different types of sea creatures.

If the natural realm is vast, how vast do you think the spiritual realm is? The natural realm consists of the earth, the solar system, and the entire universe which is actually still expanding. All of this is massive. The Godhead (Heavenly Father, Jesus, and Holy Spirit) is even bigger than that. The Bible tells us that earth is "the footstool" of the LORD (Isaiah 66:1, Acts 7:49, and Matthew 5:35). Well, the spiritual realm is much larger than the natural realm. The spiritual realm was here long before the natural realm. God created it all. There was nothing made without God. God supplied the materials, the ability to think, and the ability to create.

Apparently, the demonic kingdom has multiple kingdoms as well within its kingdom of darkness. Of these kingdoms of darkness, most believers are only familiar with the marine kingdom (think about how most of the movies made featuring underwater realms abound in evil). However, there are other demonic kingdoms operating against people. Just know that the kingdoms of Satan are all working to get the souls of men. In Revelation 18, it mentions that Babylon the great is fallen. The Babylonian empire itself consisted of many kingdoms. Like the Roman empire, it included many nations and kings that were under the rulership of Caesar. Jesus said a kingdom divided against itself cannot stand (Matthew 12:25, Mark 3:24 and Luke 11:17). When Jesus died on the cross, was resurrected, and ascended to heaven, He took back the dominion that had been established by God in the beginning. When Jesus ascended on high, he "led captivity captive" (Ephesians 4:8). These were places where the enemy had taken spiritual territory. The term captivity refers to any place of bondage or place where people are held against their will, so not every soul is locked up in the Marine kingdom. Jesus took control of everything and every location. Jesus has the right to give these keys to whom He chooses because He took back the keys of hell and death from Satan (Revelation 1:18).

As she started my nephew's deliverance, Lauren discerned that his soul was no longer present in his body. The demons said that his soul was split into multiple kingdoms. Although this may sound far-fetched at first, this is very much possible and is even mentioned in the bible. David prayed in Psalm 7:2, "Lest he tear my soul like a lion, rending *it* in pieces, while *there is* none to deliver." The devil is like a roaring lion seeking whom he may devour (1 Peter 5:8). The soul can be taken. There are multiple scriptures that validate this. What does it profit a man to gain the whole world and lose his soul (Mark 8:36 and Matthew 16:26)? The Bible also tells us: "Let the enemy persecute my soul and take *it*; yea, let him tread down my life upon the earth, and lay mine honour in the dust (Psalm 7:5, KJV)". According to the demons possessing my nephew, the marine kingdom had a portion of his soul, and another demonic kingdom had another portion. They refused to tell us any more than that. Lauren replied, "There are four demonic kingdoms. Where do you have the other part of his soul?" Both Lauren and her daughter could also see in the spirit. After this, the demon stopped acting out and caused my nephew's body to lie down.

Meanwhile, I was praying in the spirit. I was trying to understand why this was happening to us. I understand that this entire situation seems crazy and like some type of movie. The devil has been programming people to see demonic stuff as only occurring in fairy tales and made-up stories. For people who don't understand the things of the spirit, it will seem like this is a fake story. It is as if the entire world is under a spell and refusing to believe the devil even exists, while the devil is laughing and capturing souls of children. However, in truth Jesus has the first, middle, and final say. Jesus is the Alpha and Omega. Jesus was already at the end of this story.

The Lord told the deliverance minister where my nephew's soul was located. She found out that part of his soul was indeed taken to the marine kingdom. After that, things started to get really intense. The evil spirits started messing with technology again. They would mess with the TVs and the phone. The TV would come on or change channels, and the phone would go out. The demonic spirit called to Satan for help once again. My nephew's mouth even started speaking in demonic tongues. Lauren said that there was only one other deliverance during which she had heard that happened. "Sy, you need to ask Isaiah what he is into. Someone doesn't just start speaking in demonic tongues." Meanwhile, her daughter saw a vision of Isaiah's soul locked up in prison. After this, Lauren prayed that God would send an angel with her daughter to retrieve his soul. Her daughter sounded like she was only about 9 years old. Her daughter said, "Okay, Mommie." She described to us what she saw, "Mommie, I see Isaiah crying for help and he is locked up in prison. I unlocked the prison doors. We are leaving." The angel of the Lord was with her. Isaiah began to make swimming motions.

Afterwards, Isaiah was coherent and his eyes looked normal once again. Lauren said, "Watch Win Worley's video on deliverance right away." His soul was back in his body but there were still demonic spirits in there that needed to be cast out. My sister was so excited to have him back that she did not watch the video. She took him to get some smoothies instead. While in the car, she took a picture of him and sent it to me. Then, she texted saying, "Look at his eyes. Isaiah is himself again!" She began to see his personality again. He had no memory of the last 2-3 years of his life. He didn't even know that he had another little brother. His soul had been captured before my sister was pregnant with her last child. When she came back from getting smoothies with Isaiah, my nephew seemed normal, but we still needed to watch those deliverance videos.

My phone rang and it was a friend from back home in St. Louis. I answered the phone. I told her some of what had happened, and she said that the spirit was still there. While on the phone with me, she saw it. The moment she said that my nephew started acting like he was swimming again. The demons then said, "We have your place surrounded. You cannot fight thousands of us. If you cast out one, we have more that can replace them. Look outside your window. We are coming to take him back." I got off the phone with my friend. This time, the demonic spirits were completely enraged.

This time there were many days of little sleep, little food, and many hours of physically restraining him. I told the Lord Jesus, "I don't know how long I can continue with this." I knew this was straight from the devil. I warned his mother multiple times concerning the importance of her salvation as well as that of her children. I prayed and fasted while watching her go on a "roller coaster ride" of salvation. The Lord used me multiple times to warn my family. Each time, my family would run to me to fight their spiritual battles while they continued to enjoy the temptations of the world.

By now I was having a serious conversation with God. I made sure to not utter a single word of my conversation out loud. I told my sister and her family, "Let's pray and read the Word together." As soon as I began to pray, that evil spirit would take over my nephew. He grabbed my niece's Bible and began to rip the pages of out of it. The evil spirit would say, "I hate children." Then, it would make my nephew go after me to attack me. I would wrestle him to the ground and start calling on the name of Jesus. I would begin praying in the spirit. This lasted for over 12 hours until I had sweat dripping down on me and my clothes were saturated again.

During the entire ordeal, the Holy Spirit gave me supernatural strength. The Holy Spirit wouldn't let the demon overpower me. My sister was holding his legs down. Once when she let go, he kicked a hole in my bedroom door. The Lord reminded me how important it was to not get in my flesh; the flesh would simply empower that demonic spirit. After I stopped holding him, he got up. My sister said something to him, and he punched her in the face, giving her a black eye. For a moment, I got in my flesh, and he punched me in the face. However, I didn't feel the hit and it did not leave a mark.

After he punched me, my sister lost it. She started choking him to the ground. It looked like anger completely took over her. Once he was on the ground, I looked into his eyes, and I was surprised when I saw my nephew's eyes. The demons got out of the way. He looked so helpless. It was like he wanted to die. He didn't want to hit us. He had never raised his hand to us. I told my sister to stop choking him. The demon asked, "Will you kill your son?" Then Isaiah said, "Kill me, so I do not hurt you all." I kept praying.

I asked the Holy Spirit, "What should I do?" He told me to call the police and have him committed. I thought, "LORD, I don't want to give up on him." The LORD told me that I wasn't giving up on him. He told me, "You need to rest. You are spiritually and physically worn out. You need time to regain your strength. This will give you time." I trusted God so I called the police. At that very moment, the demons went down and my nephew was coherent.

When the police arrived, Isaiah talked to them. He told the police that he had demons. I knew it was spiritual but to the police it appeared to be a "mental episode". I thank God for having the right police show up that day. They appeared to have compassion for the situation. They did not want him to ride in the police car because he was so young. The policewoman said, "We can trail you to the mental hospital." We told them, "It would be safer if he rode in the police car." The police didn't want him to feel like he was in trouble. However, they agreed to let him ride in the police car. My sister and I followed them to the mental hospital. Upon arrival, my sister went inside the hospital with my nephew. She then came back outside with my nephew. She told me,

"This hospital had to turn away 15 children tonight because they reached their capacity." I said, "What!" Apparently, there were many children that night that had violent mental outbreaks.

The devil is really after these children, I thought. Then, I remembered the evil spirit saying that he hates children. There is a demonic end-time mandate to take out children. Just like during the time of Jesus' birth when Herod killed all the children two years and under. There is a mighty move of God that is going to come out of this generation, and the devil is "hell bent" on taking them out or at the very least silencing them.

We drove 30 minutes farther out from where we lived, and we finally reached a hospital that had the ability to admit him. My sister had him admitted to the mental hospital while I waited in the car. As soon as I crossed the door when we finally returned home, I went right to sleep. I had only an hour before it was time to go to work.

Chapter Twelve

Rest from the Fight

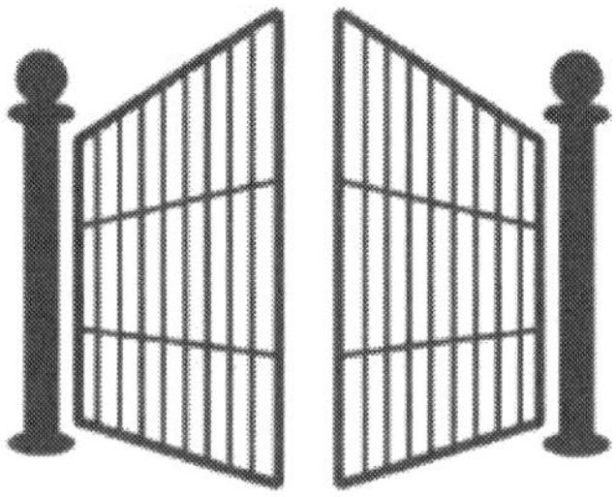

The night my nephew was admitted to the mental hospital I went straight into a dream when I finally lay down to sleep. While dreaming, I could see a woman enter my apartment. I woke up out of that dream and immediately knew something was wrong. My sister and the other three kids were still asleep. I began to get ready for work. I hadn't really gotten much sleep, but I somehow felt rested. I went ahead and logged in for work.

While working, I received a call from a friend. This was the first time I'd had a chance to talk in a while. As we talked, I told her a witch astral projected into my apartment the previous night. My friend who is prophetic said, "I heard the Lord say, your neighbor is a Wiccan." I replied, "My God, this is confirmation!" Prior to that experience, I had never seen this neighbor. This is why I did not recognize her in my dream.

Within a period of a few months, I had 3 different neighbors living above my apartment. Something seemed off with all of them.

The first neighbor had an angry look on her face when I saw her going upstairs. While she was going up the stairs, she had her cat gripped by the neck. Why is she holding her cat like that? She was gone within two weeks of me moving in. I had never seen my new neighbor, but I would hear banging on the ceiling between 2-3AM almost every night. The banging sounded like someone hitting the walls or falling on the floor. It was like they did not sleep. It was a woman and a man living above me at this time.

When I got off the phone with my friend, I began working on some assignments for work. My niece woke up and immediately told me about a dream she'd had that night. She told me that she seen a white woman with blondish hair come into my house. On her way out of the door in that dream, my niece had tried to throw something at her. The Lord dropped into my spirit that the strange woman was looking for my nephew. After my niece told me that, I received a follow-up call from Lauren, the lady who had done deliverance on my nephew. She wanted to know what had happened after we took my nephew to the mental hospital. She hadn't wanted us to take him to the hospital at the time. Lauren had explained, "I don't want him to think you all don't love him." I told her that I was tired and needed some rest from the incessant spiritual and physical battle.

At the time there seemed to be a strong legal right for those evil spirits to stay there in my nephew's body. Lauren told me that a witch was interfering with the deliverance of Isaiah. She asked me, "What do you know about your neighbor that stays above you?" I told her, "I have never seen her before." I told her that I thought she was a witch based on many separate confirmations. I told her that while I was on the phone with a friend, she had heard the Lord say that my neighbor was a Wiccan. Lauren simply said, "A Wiccan is a witch." She gave me a book to read by a Christian doctor who had helped a woman leave the occult. I only had time to listen to it audibly. She told me, "This is what you are going through." During my nephew's deliverance, there had been witches surrounding the apartment. It was like there was an army of them.

While listening to the book, I learned that I was not crazy and this stuff really happens. Witches can interfere with deliverance. Some witches can even control the body of someone that has been given over to Satan. How do you handle a human spirit of someone who chooses to be a witch versus a demonic spirit? Witches do not always stop "in the name of Jesus" because they have free-will just like you and I. This explained all the different personalities that I had encountered while trying to get my nephew free. It had been like I was talking to different men and women. According to the Word of God, you can cast out a demon in the name of Jesus. However, humans have free will and are still redeemable. This is why cutting the silver cord which tethers their spirit and soul to their body is the only option in some cases. However, you **must** be led by the Holy Spirit to do this because to cut their silver cord is to kill them.

I had been busy trying to tell a demon to come out in the name of Jesus, but witches and warlocks were interfering. After listening to the book, my eyes were opened. I didn't even know that any of that stuff was possible before my experiences and listening to the book. Without that book, I would have thought 'this sounds crazy and unbelievable.' When Isaiah's mother found out that a witch was interfering to block him from being set free, she wanted to handle it the "street way". My sister said, "I am about to go up there and knock her out." I told my sister, "You can't fight or win a spiritual battle in a carnal way. Right now, we have the protection of the Lord." Yea though I walk through the valley of the shadow of death, I will fear no evil for God is with me (Psalm 23).

My niece left the apartment to take a walk because she was also mad. While my niece was out walking, she saw my upstairs neighbor. When she came back into the apartment, she said: "I came across your upstairs neighbor, and she looks just like the lady in my dream." This was the first time she had ever seen her. This neighbor was the one that had astral projected into my apartment. She was looking for my nephew. I remembered the vision my friend had where she saw an army of angels in armor coming to help me. During all the spiritual warfare, the Lord of Hosts was protecting and fighting for us. Lord Jesus helped me himself! Therefore, no man can take His glory. Why would the LORD Himself help me? The answer to that question is: Why not you? God used Gideon's army of just 300 souls to defeat a nation of Midianites. God made even the weakest of His creation in His own image and likeness. The Lord Jesus Himself carried the weight of this spiritual battle that I found myself in. I would have never made it without Jesus.

I used the time while my nephew was in the hospital to refresh. I had wanted to fast, however, an older saint who I trusted advised against it. She told me, "You need to eat meat and regain your physical strength." I realized then that I had paid to attend a conference out of town in Houston. The Children's Mental Hospital was only keeping Isaiah until they felt it was safe to release him. So far, the evil spirits have been playing with the doctors. Demons are highly intelligent ancient beings. This is why we need the wisdom of the Holy Spirit. My sister had been keeping in contact with the hospital concerning her son, Isaiah, and his progress. According to the doctors, he would be ready to be released soon. Everything seemed to be going well. I asked, "Holy Spirit, what should I do? Should I go to that Christian business conference? Should

I stay?" I heard in my spirit, "Go, and trust me." I went to the conference and left them in God's hands.

I finally got a chance to go to sleep without looking over my shoulder or being on high spiritual alert. Every time my nephew had gotten up from the couch and come towards my room, I immediately woke up. I would catch him standing in the doorway. One of the things that kept me going and suffering for so long was that I knew that it was not really my nephew. My sister said she wanted to go visit my nephew at the hospital. I also wanted to see how he was doing so I decided to go with her the next day. As for tonight, I thought, "Lord, let me get a good night of rest."

Chapter Thirteen

Understanding the Real Battle

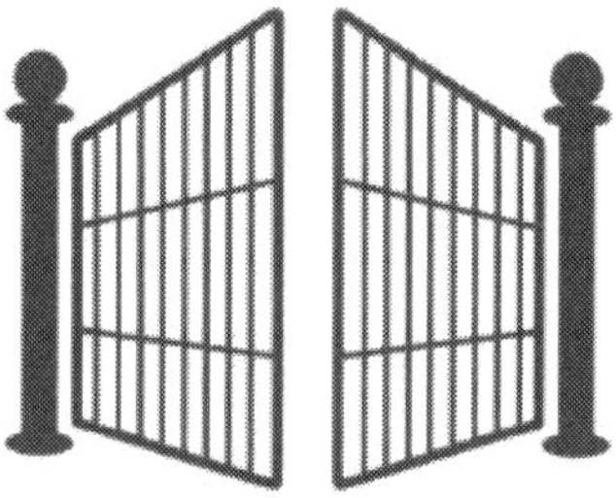

During daybreak, I woke up to pray. After prayer, I got ready for work. Oh, my goodness, today was the weekend for the conference in Houston. I had totally lost track of time. I don't usually work on weekends. 'Let me get some things done,' I thought. I cleaned my place and washed my clothes. Then I began researching on my phone, looking for any similar situations to the one we had been experiencing with Isaiah. I decided to use my time wisely and finished reading the book on deliverance that Lauren had recommended. Some of things I read seemed to resonate with my spirit. Wow, the author really went through a lot to help this one lady get out of the occult. There were so many things

I wanted to ask Lauren. She had personal experiences with the occult herself because of her family and her own child.

Finally, it was approaching the time to go see my nephew. I asked my sister, "So, what is the status?" Roz replied, "Isaiah seems to be doing well, and they could be releasing him soon." She then asked me if I was ready to go. I said, "Yes, let me just get my purse." I drove to the hospital. Once we entered the building, they asked us for ID. I noticed as soon as I got into the building, that it felt very spiritually dark in there. We sat down and waited for Isaiah. When he came out, he seemed to be medicated. It still didn't seem like him though. Isaiah began to tell us about the fights that happened there. He also said that some of the kids were doing witchcraft. I saw another young boy that looked about 10 years old. I could tell that child was extremely demonized. Isaiah simply commented, "That boy likes to play video games."

Instantly a thought came to my mind. Could video games be the root cause for this child's mental issues and demonization? It was an eerie feeling at that mental hospital. I could really feel a strong demonic presence. Isaiah seemed so calm, but the medicine also made him seem spaced out. You cannot medicate a demon. Our visit didn't last that long, maybe 30 minutes. The whole time it was as if we were talking to someone else. Isaiah's personality wasn't there. We went back home. I remember thinking how much he needed Jesus, the savior and deliverer.

What's next, I wondered? I needed to prepare for my trip to Houston in a few days. I had already paid for it, and I was not going to let the enemy stop me. I thought back to one of the things which had happened with Isaiah while they were still in St. Louis. My cell phone had rung and it was Rae calling me. She told me, "It is Isaiah." It sounded like she was outside. "What is wrong?" I asked. Rae told me, "He beat Elijah up badly. Elijah has marks all over his body. Isaiah claims he is a demon. I had to grab Melo from the crib and get Elijah. Then, I ran out of the house. Can you come and get us?" She sounded desperate. I asked Rae, "Where are you?" "I am at the 7 eleven down the street. Isaiah is following us on his bike. I am scared, Sy. He hurt Elijah bad."

Rae continued to say, "Sy, we look a mess. Melo only has on a pamper with no shoes on. Elijah has his clothes on backwards." The 7-Eleven manager took one look at them and called the police. Then the phone began to go in and out. "What Rae?" I asked. "I cannot hear you." The phone connection broke up, and I could only hear static. "Rae, Hello!" I shouted. Rae said, "What? He got you too, he is controlling the phones." Then the phone disconnected. 'Lord Jesus, what is going on?' I wondered. She did not tell me where they were. Let me call their mother, Roz. The phone rang and her voicemail picked up. "This is important. Roz call me back!" I said on her voicemail. My phone soon rang with my sister calling me back. "Where are you? Your kids need you." I said when I answered her call. Roz said, "I am on my way now." When Roz got there, the police were questioning Rae. Roz walked up and said, "I am the mother." The police replied, "This child has current bruises, he needs to go the hospital. Your son, Isaiah, told us that Rae beat on them." "What?" said Roz, not believing what the police were telling her. She looked at Elijah, and it looked bad. He looked like he had been beaten like a slave.

Roz said, "I don't believe my daughter did this." Rae was 18 years old at the time. The police walked over to Elijah and asked him, "Who did this to you?" Elijah said, "It was Isaiah that did this to me." They then took Elijah to the hospital. "Roz, what happened? I couldn't quite understand Rae because the phone kept messing up." I spoke. My sister replied, "Sy, I am on my way to the hospital now." I will call you back later to let you know what happens."

I began praying. "Lord Jesus, I know you said to stop praying for her because she made her choice and walked away from you. Lord, please have mercy on her children." I was a 10-hour drive away from St. Louis now. My phone finally rang. "Hi, Roz. How is Elijah?" She replied, "Let me send you a picture; he has marks all over his body." I said, "My God, this picture looks bad. Isaiah did that to Elijah? That had to be a demon working through him." My sister told me, "Sy, Child Protective Services has been called. I just finished talking to them. Elijah and Isaiah cannot stay in the same house. Can you keep Isaiah?" I replied, "I have a planned trip to Washington, D.C. and Baltimore. Can someone else take him until I get back?" She replied, "Sy, I asked certain family members. They said no. If you don't keep him, Elijah could be taken by CPS and be kept in the system." I asked her, "Could I keep Elijah instead of Isaiah?" She replied, "I will bring him down there to you."

Chapter Fourteen
The Dream Gate

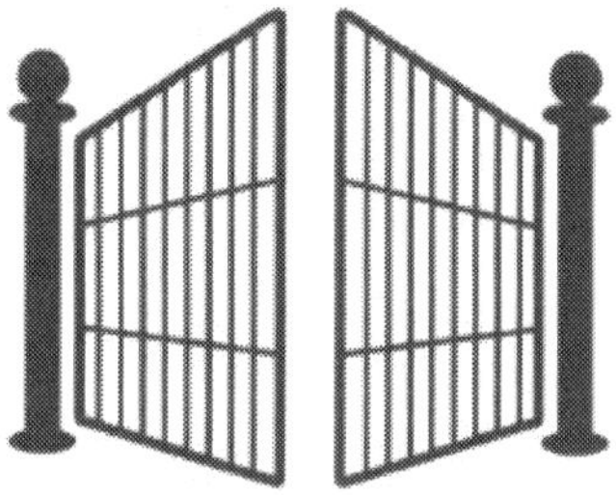

While I was still trying to get a revelation from the Lord of how to help Isaiah, I remembered a dream I had years ago. During the dream, I went to my sister's apartment to warn her to get out. She took her time and was not moving fast enough. While she was still getting out of bed, her boyfriend and his friends came and shot her. I was telling her, let's go, but she did not listen.

I woke up from that dream and began praying and then told my sister the next day to be careful. I had that same dream twice. In the second dream, my sister moved a little faster and we made it to the door. Once we got to the door though, they busted in the door and started shooting. While in the dream, I was behind the door watching.

Dreams are so important. God mentions dreams all throughout the Bible. Joseph, the husband of Mary, was warned by an angel of the Lord in a dream to go to Egypt because King Herod wanted the kill their baby, Jesus. The fact that the dream I had about my sister happened twice was letting me know that it was going to happen and that it was an important warning. The Word says that by two or three witnesses let every word be established (2 Corinthians 13:1). At the time of this dream, I had no idea about how to cancel dreams and destroy altars through spiritual warfare. I was ignorant. God said his people perish for a lack of knowledge (Hosea 4:6). I didn't have the revelation of who the dream was about. It turned out that the dream was not really about my sister, but rather it was a warning about my cousin.

On Christmas day of that year, I was at home. My phone rang and I answered it. My mom said, "They can't find Reese (my cousin)." She asked me to pray. I started praying but didn't have any peace. Something just didn't feel right. At the time, I was not where I was supposed to be with the Lord. I was being spiritually distracted by the man from Seattle. After 15 years of waiting on God for His promises and for the salvation of my family, I had grown weary. I was fighting strong demonic forces by myself, and I had no one to turn to for help. We really need community as Christians no matter how long we have walked with the Lord. No one can win a war alone. Yet another reason why Jesus called us the Body of Christ.

After the initial phone call with my mom, I was waiting to hear something more. My phone rang and I quickly answered the phone. My sister said, "Reese is dead! He killed her." I said, "What?!" Next, my mom called on my other line. I answered the other line, "Reese's car was outside. The police did a wellness check. Then, all the police showed up. We couldn't get into the house. The police asked how many children Reese had. We told them three." The baby had been murdered, and her two other children were missing. The baby didn't belong to her husband who she was separated from. Apparently, he killed the baby and took his children with him when he left. He had just been released from a five-year prison sentence for kidnapping her before.

While all of this was going on, we still did not know what had happened to her. Apparently, God had warned her after she had been kidnapped. A lady from Church had said to her, "How long did you want to live?" She didn't respond. After the kidnapping, the police had even warned her, "If someone tells you: 'If I can't have you, no one will,' believe them because they will kill you." Unfortunately, when he was released from prison, she started speaking to him again. That reconnection led to her death. During the funeral, I could not even stand up and view the body. I was so concerned about where her soul went.

I picked up a spirit of grief from this tragedy, and I now believe it was an open door leading to the wrong relationship for me. During the time of my cousin's murder, I met the man from Seattle online. It was a test of my foundation. My foundation was not stable. Build your foundation on the rock of Jesus Christ. Submit all your hurts to God. When mourning turns into an extended time of grief, in my experience, this can become an open door for the devil.

Chapter Fifteen

Generational Gates

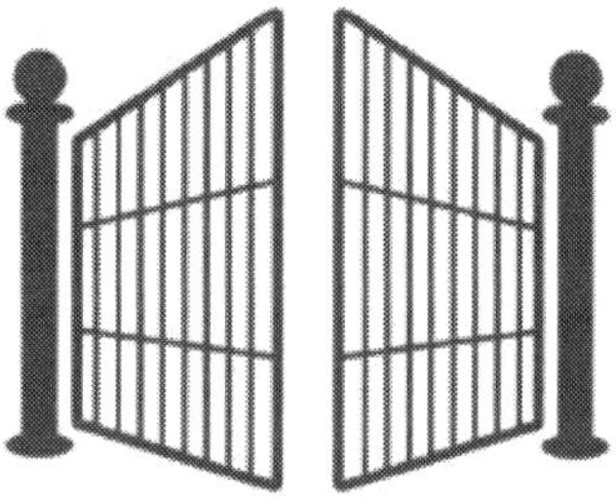

I looked outside and the sun was shining so brightly. I needed the light of the Lord Jesus concerning this situation. What was the root of it? Why was my nephew so demonized? When Jesus came to a tree that did not bear fruit, He cursed it at the root. As I pondered what the root of this situation could be, a childhood memory flashed in my mind. I remembered it as if it had happened just yesterday. I sat in the back seat of my mom's car as it moved down the highway. As I gazed out of the car window, I asked my mom, "Where are we going?" My mom said, "We are going to Big Daddy's funeral in Memphis." After a five-hour drive, we finally made it there and took seats inside the church. We made it just in time. As soon as we sat down, it was time to get up and look at the body. Before we even made it to the casket, a woman let out a loud scream and fell on the casket. As I looked at the man lying in the casket,

I didn't remember ever seeing him before. I did not know what to think as we exited out the door of the Church.

My mom told my aunt, "We are going to follow you to the burial site." My aunt said, "Okay." As we left the church parking lot, we were being escorted by police in front, along the sides, and at the back of the procession. All the people pulled their cars over to the side of the road as the funeral procession passed to show respect for the deceased. Who was my great granddad? The funeral was extravagant and there were so many people there. They were really making a big deal out of this funeral, I thought. My grandmom said, "He was a mason for so many years." This one memory ended up being the key to breakthrough for my immediate family. Isaiah's father was also currently a mason. We had that generational curse on both sides of the family, through both bloodlines.

These secret societies have negative generational impact. Have you noticed evil patterns in your family? Membership in the secret society of the masons explained many of the bad patterns within my family. My grandmom said, "Oh, it is a good organization. They help a lot of people get ahead and do a lot for the community." A "good" thing is not always a God thing. I am sure Lucifer thought it was a "good" thing when he led a third of the angels out of heaven in rebellion. By being in the masons, my great grandfather tied his descendants to evil altars and evil covenants that it would take years to break. It seriously took years for breakthrough. It was years without progress, not because the power of Jesus Christ was not strong enough to break it. The demonic strongholds had a legal right to harass and attack our family through the covenantal vows and oaths that were made by my grandfather within the masons. It was his lack of knowledge about the effects of those vows that he made that caused some family members to even die prematurely.

It appeared that the women of our family were more of a target then the men. Some of the women in my family experienced molestation or rape. It was almost as if there was a target on the women. They attracted occultic men. The men all seemed to be in or connected to some type of secret society. It was like the women were hidden from righteous men and only attracted the types of men who were in the masons or other secret societies. The women did not join those secret societies themselves but would marry men that were a part of them. If the men were not a part of them, the marriages would not last long.

Idolatry is a destroyer of destinies. The word idol-a-try breaks apart as if to say, "let me try an idol before I try God." However, the Bible specifically warns us, "Thou shalt not bow down thyself to them (idols or other gods), nor serve them: for I the LORD thy God *am* a jealous God, visiting the iniquity of the fathers upon the children unto the third and fourth *generation* of them that hate me; And shewing mercy unto thousands of them that love me, and keep my commandments." (Exodus 20:5-6) In our family, the enemy was attempting to re-establish a covenant in the fifth generation. The use of the word "visiting" implies that each generation has a way out. If you don't kick that visitor (generational iniquity) out, it will keep coming back throughout the generations.

Let us look at the family history of Moses to examine the effects of iniquity across generations. Levi begot Kohath who begot Amram and Amram begot Moses. In other words, Levi was the great grandfather of Moses. Unfortunately, Jacob cursed his son, Levi, with a spirit of anger (Genesis 49:5-7). Levi broke a blood covenant out of anger when he killed his sister's rapist who had become her husband (Genesis 34:7). Levi felt justified in his actions, and was unremorseful and unrepentant. Can you blame him? However, there was still a covenant and an agreement that had been made with the Hivites. Yet Simeon and Levi killed a whole nation out of anger. The problem was that they broke covenant through their angry actions as well as breaking the commandment against idolatry. In that moment, Levi and Simeon served the god of anger. Furthermore, they disobeyed God by joining themselves with another nation and then by breaking that blood covenant with the Hivites. They made a blood covenant with the Hivites to leave them in a vulnerable position to be murdered while they were recovering from being circumcised to join with the women of Israel. This blood covenant went directly against the Lord's instructions and adversely affected the whole nation of Israel until a deliver was raised up. The whole nation went from the place of Goshen to a place of bondage by the third generation after Levi. The curse of having a spirit of anger had a direct impact on Moses as well, three generations later. The enemy knows that if the one making the evil covenant sees problems right away that they could possibly discover the source of their issues. It is the generations that come afterwards that must truly search to find out why they are experiencing opposition and/or oppression. It is family secrets that keep generations in bondage. We need to have a candid conversation with our children and grandchildren about the family generational sins.

We must offer ourselves up as a living sacrifice (Romans 12:1). Jesus' ultimate sacrifice led to the deliverance of the world. Oftentimes, we only focus on our own issues and family. However, our freedom is also connected to the freedom of others. Your salvation and deliverance will not only help your bloodline, but it can also help a nation of other people.

Chapter Sixteen

THE ROOT OF THE PROBLEM

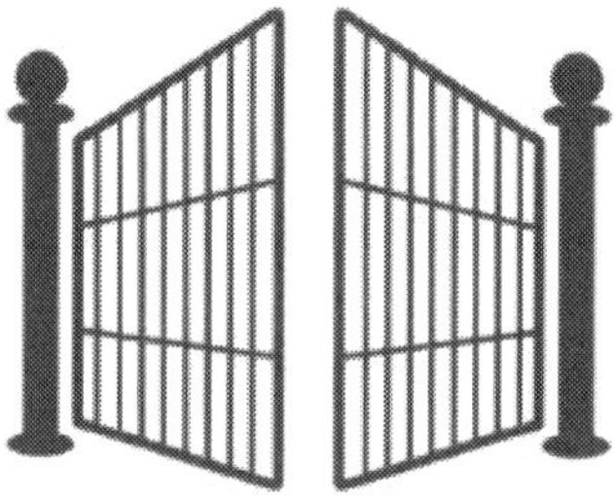

The Bible tells us, "The Lord said, If ye had faith as a grain of mustard seed, ye might say unto this sycamine tree, Be thou plucked up by the root, and be thou planted in the sea; and it should obey you." (Luke 17:6, KJV) So I was puzzled when all the attempts at deliverance for my nephew failed to be successful. However, right before this scripture about faith, Jesus was discussing forgiveness with His disciples. Unforgiveness causes roots to grow deep and twisted, making it impossible to uproot them without the help of God. Unforgiveness is a major blockage to a person receiving deliverance. The Bible also warns, "But if ye do not forgive, neither will your Father which is in heaven forgive your trespasses" (Mark 11:26, KJV). Did you notice that within this scripture the writer referred to God as our Father in Heaven? You may ask "Why?" I believe this is because unforgiveness will keep you from entering heaven. If so, being demonized because of unforgiveness could in reality be God's mercy shown to you while you still have time to repent and forgive others while still on earth. The key is to pluck unforgiveness out by the root.

To get to the roots of unforgiveness, you are going to have to become like a detective. A detective is an investigator, usually some sort of member of a law enforcement agency. During the deliverance process it was revealed that my nephew (age 11) had unforgiveness towards a young man that had bullied him at school. It is important to completely educate your children. A child can really struggle with the concept of unforgiveness. Our society makes us think that by forgiving someone we are saying that what they did to us was okay. Not the case. The truth is that we are really choosing to no longer let a bad experience from the past continue to mess with us in the present. If unforgiveness is not dealt with, it can take deep root within our hearts. The devil does not play fair. He does not care about age. If the devil could get you while you were still in the womb, he would. When we asked Isaiah to forgive the one who had bullied him, my nephew did not even understand what forgiveness was.

There will be times when you will have to do some deeper investigation in order to help others find freedom. Detectives often collect information to solve crimes by talking to witnesses and searching databases. The good news is that you do not have to do this all on your own, the Holy Spirit gives you divine intelligence. We have every right through the blood of Jesus Christ to enforce His law against the devil. Our "database" for finding freedom for the oppressed is the Word of God. If you start to ask your family some questions, you will begin to see patterns. Those patterns are indicators of a root issue. The key is getting to the root. It is time to ask questions.

Chapter Seventeen

The End-Times Connection

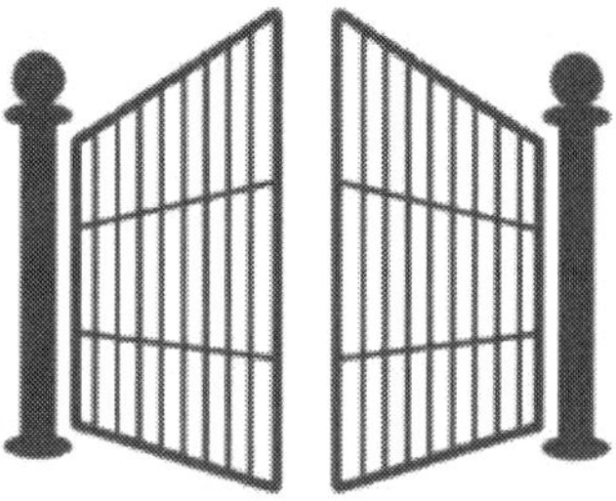

Wake up! It was time to go to war on my knees once again. Jesus, what should I do? My nephew was about to be released from the mental hospital. Could I leave my sister here to fight this alone? I had a business conference to go to. I had already bought the tickets and they were not cheap, yet they would be worth it. I had booked the hotel. I heard the Lord say, "Go." It was extremely hard to focus on business when I felt like I was still in the middle of World War 3 in my own home.

I drove three hours to get to the place where the conference was going to be held, and was physically and spiritually exhausted. As I was standing in the line, I looked at the people and it looked like they were still in the "matrix" of self. However, I was there. I was going to Church while the enemy was having a field day with my family. We were at war and the enemy had launched an all-out attack against the children within my family. The devil is also after your children, grandchildren, nieces, and nephews. If not your family, what about your next-door neighbor's children?

As I sat down at the conference, I was so glad I came. It was more than I had expected. It was not just another business or Christian business conference. It was a three-day conference event. On one of the days, the speaker was even talking about deliverance. What got my attention was the section on soul captivity - this was what was going on with my nephew. The speaker began to administer a mass deliverance session. As she called out a spirit, the lady next to me fell to the ground, screaming and coughing up stuff. The same thing was happening all over the place within the conference hall. The next day, I was at the altar when the speaker was preaching. She prophesied that "in 24 hours your situation will turn around." I **knew** that word was for me.

At the end of the conference, I went back to the hotel and prepared myself to leave in the morning. My phone rang. It was my sister. "Hi, is everything ok?" I asked. My sister said, "Yes!" I began to hear the excitement in her voice. She continued, "Let me tell you what happened." After she picked my nephew up from the hospital, they all went straight to a revival service. Roz said, "I had Rae, Elijah, Isaiah and Melo all with me. When we arrived in the parking lot, Isaiah did not want to get out of the car. We forced him to get out of the car. We sat down in the service, and Isaiah told me he had to go to the restroom. While in the foyer of the Church, a man walked up to him and Isaiah punched him. The man and a 13-year-old boy then took Isaiah to the back to do deliverance on him. While I was sitting down in the service, someone asked me to come to the back of the building concerning my son." My sister went back there. They were administering deliverance to him. My nephew threw a punch toward the men. They were back there for about an hour. As the man laid his hand on Isaiah's chest, he did not feel a heartbeat. The man asked me questions. "I told him, "His soul was held captive in the marine kingdom." He said, "Okay." Roz continued to tell me, "They prayed and continued to administer deliverance. Suddenly, it looked like Isaiah had come back to his body. As he lay there, his heart started beating fast. I called Isaiah's name. The man who had been leading the deliverance asked him, 'How old are you?' Isaiah said, 'I am eight years old.' I said, 'No, he is eleven.' When the deliverance was done, the service was just about over."

My sister continued, "As we went back to the car, Isaiah asked 'who is this'? He did not even recognize his two-year-old brother." He had no memory of 3 whole years of his life on earth. I began to praise God. Then, I asked my sister, "Where are you now?" She replied, "We are headed home."

While I was still on the phone with my sister, my nephew had a vision. He began to share his vision; it was an end-time vision about the last days on Earth. He saw himself left behind. He also started to remember other visions he had before he lost his memory. In the vision, Jesus was on one side, and Satan was on the other side. He was in the middle. I said to my sister, "We are going to have to finish this conversation later on." After I got off the phone with them, I was amazed at how God had come through for us all. Night after night, my nephew had been standing over my sister and niece while they were sleeping. They would wake up to him just standing over them. There is power in prayer. Death could be staring you in the face, but when Jesus has the keys, all death can do is stare. It cannot touch you because of Jesus Christ. All glory to God.

Chapter Eighteen

The Legal Right

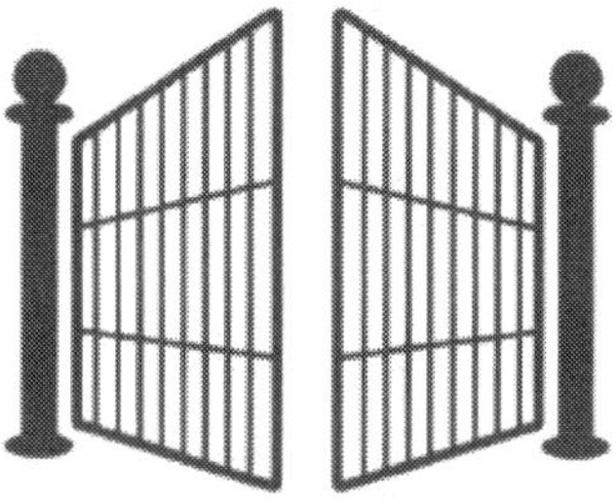

I woke up in my own bed the day after the conference ended and I had heard the wonderful news from my sister about Isaiah finally being delivered. Peace. There is nothing like peace, and I am not just talking about internal peace. The atmosphere of my home was now peaceful again. Jesus, I thank you. The thought flashed through my head, "You need to ask your nephew some questions. No one just suddenly starts speaking in demonic tongues and calling on Satan to help them." I became a detective on assignment. The moment my nephew wakes up, he needs to start talking, I thought. For three years, his mom talked to demons and not him. For the first night since they had arrived in Texas, I had not woken up to him standing at my door. He did not always come to my room, sometimes he would just be wide awake, just sitting on the couch. He did not seem to ever really sleep. This morning, it looked like he was catching up on years of sleepless nights. Let him rest I thought, then we will talk. It was the middle of the day when he finally woke up. "Hi, Isaiah," I greeted him. He replied, "Hi, Sy." "How did you sleep?" I asked. He said, "I slept good." I told him that I needed to ask him some things. "Okay," he said. "What happened to you?" I asked, and then I continued to tell him, "I am here to listen, no judgement. It is safe to talk." My nephew began to explain his experience.

This is what he said happened. "I was introduced to witchcraft for a time and learned things through a video game. I also learned from my teacher at school how to sell my soul. The video game also taught me some witchcraft. During that time, I was being bullied by the kids at my school. Then, Satan appeared to me when I was 8 years old with a contract. He said, 'If you sell your soul, I will give you power and friends.' I said, 'Yes.' Then, I was snatched out of my body. Demons came in to act as me. I would hear them from another place calling my mom, 'mom'." Warning to parents, please get involved with your children. If you cannot home school them, get to know their teachers and friends. Monitor them while they play video games. If possible, do not let them play video games at all. The video games today are not like the video games of the past. It is designed to keep them addicted and unfruitful. Time is our greatest asset, and the devil is teaching them how to waste it. The devil sends his agents to schools and to the video game world to catch unguarded children. Will you please protect your children from demons who need a host?

As his mom is listening, she remembered a dream encounter. During the dream, my sister was in a large empty mansion. Satan showed up and spoke via an intercom system within the mansion. The devil said, "I will give you all of this and more, if you will pray to me at 3AM every day. You can keep your bible on the table in the living room." My sister looked around and noticed she was alone. She told satan, "No!" She was then pulled out of that night vision. This encounter happened about 5 years before satan approached her son. It was not enough just to say no. She should have given her life to Jesus. She said no, but he still wanted her children. Satan's target was her children. When the parents don't slay the giants, they leave the giants to their children to fight.

My nephew told me that he went to hell and other places in the spirit realm. The first place he went to looked beautiful like Wakanda. I asked, "How do you know about Wakanda?" That movie came out after Isaiah was 8. My nephew replied, "We saw movies in hell before they were released on the earth. It was called hell because it is the abode of Satan and the kingdom of darkness. Yet, he described the place as being beautiful. There was a part of Hell where Lucifer's picture was hung everywhere. What do you expect? He is the embodiment of a narcissist.

My nephew said, "Lucifer did not get a fair shot. He was just kicked out of heaven." As he was talking, the Holy Spirit was talking to me. I replied, "The devil lied to you; he is the father of lies." God then told me to just listen; Isaiah had been indoctrinated by Luciferian doctrine for 3 years. It was going to take consistency only found in the Word of God to break those strongholds. My nephew then said, "He wants me in his end-time army." I replied, "The devil and all that follow him will be in the lake of fire to burn for eternity. (Rev 20:10,15)"

My nephew then began to tell me, "I have seen Satan in different forms. One form was beautiful. The other form was ugly, and his body was full of maggots. In the ugly form, the words that came out of Satan's mouth even looked ugly, like vomit with all kinds of nasty stuff in it. The smell was horrible. I felt sorry for him." My niece, who had been quiet for most of the time spoke out when hearing that. Rae said, "Don't feel sorry for him."

Isaiah said, "Well, the place was as beautiful as Wakanda." He continued to tell me: "He is training his army now for the end-time battle." My nephew then said, "Your neighbor upstairs takes trips to that place. It is like us being in a classroom. Lucifer was teaching us witchcraft. He is preparing witches and warlocks for the end-time battle. If they fail their assignment, they get beat up." Some of what Isaiah described could explain why some Luciferians say that it will be a party in hell. The devil has shown them an illusion, not reality. Remember, there was a party scene in the movie, "The Matrix" that referred to it as Club Hell. He mentioned seeing different types of demonic beings. One of the beings that was helping satan look like an alien.

Isaiah continued to say, "Your neighbor upstairs is doing witchcraft on you right now to kill you. She has been trying to get you. I saw her." My nephew then said, "She is going to die, because the devil is going to kill her." I immediately began to pray. I could discern truth in it. Right then, my friend who is a woman of God and a seer called me. I told her that I would call her back. I had no fear despite what Isaiah had just told me. I said out loud, "No weapon that is formed against me shall prosper; and every tongue that shall rise against me in judgment thou shalt condemn" (Isaiah 54:17). I told my nephew "No" meaning that the witch would not succeed against me. I prayed that she would repent. Let Jesus judge her.

I rarely saw this neighbor, however, I would hear movement upstairs all hours of the night. As I opened the door to go outside, she dragged her cat by the neck up the stairs. There was a broom sitting outside my door. I found out later that witches use brooms. Oddly enough, these occultic people put some occultic reality in movies. The moment that neighbor moved out, another one also involved in witchcraft moved in. This time it was a man and a woman. The spiritual warfare intensified.

They were on assignment by the enemy to take me out before complete breakthrough in Isaiah's situation. My nephew told me the demons saw me as the strongest in the family and had devised a plan to take me out. The man you met from Seattle was sent by the devil to get you out of the way. The man that is talking to Rae right now is an agent of the marine kingdom. They have a book on you all. It consists of your strengths and weaknesses. My fervent prayer is "Let that book be destroyed in the mighty name of Jesus."

I hate the devil. The devil is a copycat; he wants to be like God. The devil has a copycat system to record all of the things you do to accuse you before the courts of heaven (Job 1:6). The devil got the idea of keeping records in a book from God's Book of Life and other books he saw while he was still in heaven. There is a book in heaven with our names in it that contains details about our lives (Psalm 139:16 and Revelations 20:12). Your book in heaven needs to be unlocked so that you can walk out God's plan for your life. The Holy Bible describes Jesus as the author and finisher of our faith. Jesus is the Word of God. Imagine the Word of God writing your story. Next, imagine Him blotting out your sins and any generational iniquities when you repent of your sins and turn your life over to Him. After He removes the record of your sins from your book, He writes your name in the Lamb's Book of Life.

The Book of Life is separate from your own book. Revelation says that the dead are judged out of the things written in those books. They are judged according to their works. Works are associated with business, employment, that with which any one is occupied, industry, acts, deeds, or things done. What if Jesus has a book in which He assigned you the opportunity to do certain things (Ephesians 2:10) and you learned you would be judged based upon how you completed those assignments? We need to submit ourselves to the author and perfecter of our faith

(Hebrews 12:2) and not insist upon writing our own story. We can only maximize our impact while on the earth when we come into alignment with what Jesus has already written for each one of us.

Chapter Nineteen

THE GATE OF ENTERTAINMENT

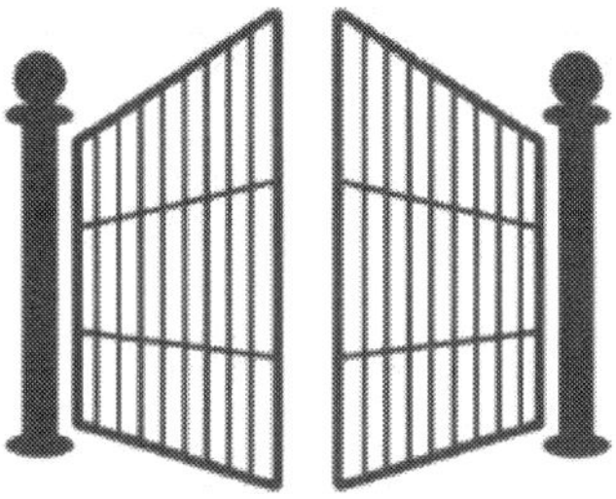

While still processing the experiences we had recently been through, I was taken back to a past memory. It was a Saturday morning, and I looked up at the television. There was a commercial playing, saying: "Yay, no school today." As the commercial finished, a movie began, starting with the credits. Across the screen it said, "Teen Wolf." The main character in this movie was a teenager. There was a scene in which the main character's team was losing the basketball game to the opposing team. The main character suddenly turned into a werewolf. Afterwards, his ability to play basketball and his popularity increased. His team won the basketball game due to his new skill at basketball. Later, he found out that he had inherited the family curse of turning into a werewolf. As a child, this movie seemed like make-believe to me and it was not considered to be a horror film but was marketed as a "coming-of-age" comedy. While in fact, it showed a dark spiritual reality as a form of entertainment.

Entertainment is a combined word: enter-tain-ment. According to the Merriam Webster dictionary, the word enter means to go or come in, to make a beginning, to begin to consider a subject, to go upon a land for the purpose of taking possession, to come on stage, to put formally on record, and to place in proper form before a court of law or upon record. The Latin root "Tain" means to hold onto something or to maintain in a specific state or condition.

I had no idea that what was depicted in the movie as childish make believe was real until I encountered it. The Bible warns us there will be wolves in sheep clothing (Matthew 7:15). While this movie appears to be innocent and light, in fact it is very demonic and dark. The Bible also warns us, "And have no fellowship with the unfruitful works of darkness but rather reprove *them*" (Ephesians 5:11). These things are strategically put into movies while the Church is ignorant so the enemy can devour our children. It has been a very effective plan of hell to get access to the minds of the children. It is called lesser magic.

Lesser magic, also known as wile and guile, refers to the practice of manipulation through applied psychology and situational awareness. It involves techniques such as using glamour, rhetoric, and strategic flattery to influence others' behaviors and secure personal advantage.

This form of magic is characterized by its everyday application and is different from greater magic, which focuses on structured rituals for the manipulation of others. What are most of today's shows and movies? Programming. This is occultic. All movies are created from a spiritual source. These movies are not just expressions of creativity and art. All creativity comes from a source and has a purpose.

Entertainment releases things (evil spirits, strongholds, and programming) to enter into the mind through the eye gates while keeping people in a state of ignorance. It has been said that Africa is known for witchcraft; I tell you that America is on a higher level than Africa concerning the use of witchcraft. The United States is the most powerful and influential nation in the world. Programming and broadcasting have this nation under a spell. While Americans are watching television, the enemy is telling-a-vision from hell. The Church seeing it as "only entertainment" causes the people to come into agreement with the satanic agenda for the world. When watching a secular movie, do not dismiss it as merely fantasy. The television has now come to our phones. We carry our phones everywhere we go. The television can be used as a portal, so can your phone. I am not saying to get rid of those items, but to be watchful. Keep your spirit guarded.

What if someone told you they saw a werewolf? Would you believe them? This is what my nephew experienced. He was being trained to turn into one. Have you ever heard of "shape shifters"? Let me assure you they are not just creatures out of someone's imagination – they are a part of the dark kingdom and they do exist. While I was wrestling with my nephew for hours on end, that thing was trying to manifest. I prayed in the spirit for over 12 hours on one occasion while I was wrestling with him. It was not by my might or power but by the Holy Spirit that I was able to stay engaged in the battle for my nephew. The Holy Spirit gave me supernational strength and angelic assistance. At the time, the evil spirits had legal rights to be there because my nephew had sold his soul through unforgiveness, his agreements, and strongholds of demonic doctrine which he had not torn down. After 12 hours of wrestling and praying in the spirit, the demonic spirit inhabiting my nephew's body finally became weaker. The demonic spirit once again said, "I am dying, Satan help me." An evil presence then filled the room and the demonic spirit began to gain strength. The demon then said, "I am leaving this house," and my nephew began to walk towards the door. I body slammed him onto the couch and said to the demonic spirit, "You are not leaving this house with my nephew's body." At the time I wondered how I was able to flip my nephew like that. God must have given me supernatural strength; it was like I truly had the spirit of might. I knew the strength that God gave Samson was real. I believe there was an angel of the Lord that made my nephew sit down on the floor there and stare at the wall all that night. At one point when satan showed up, the demon in my nephew said it saw Michael. During that time, Lauren said that she saw in the spirit, Michael fighting Satan and the Queen. The queen is mentioned in Revelation. Through it all, I trusted that God would not allow me to be touched or hurt in any way. I was even able to get some rest that night.

Chapter Twenty

THE DOTS FINALLY CONNECT

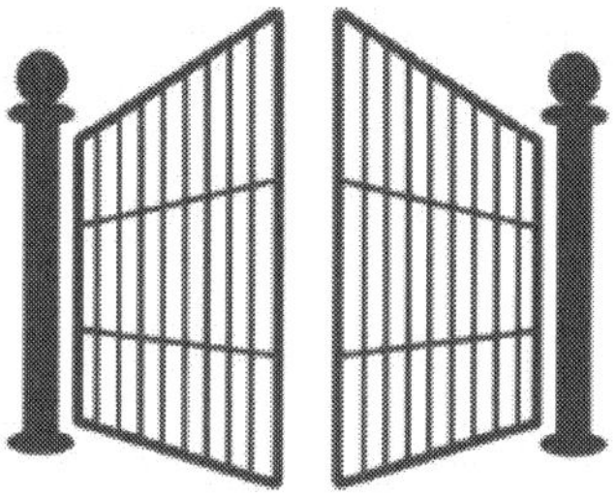

All the dots finally began to connect. While I was in Texas, there was a time when Isaiah and Elijah came up missing for a short period of time. My sister was at home when she noticed they had left the house. She got in her car to find them. She found them at the pool where she told them not to be. Isaiah and Elijah's clothes were soaked so she trailed them in her car. She told them, "I am going to whoop y'all". They took off and disappeared before her eyes. She called the police. The police searched the house and the surrounding area. They could not find Isaiah and Elijah. Then, my sister called me and our mom. I began to pray. My mom went immediately to my sister's place to help look for them. When my mom arrived, she called both of their names.

Suddenly, they appeared from behind the dumpster. My mom yelled, "I found them." The police said, "We checked that area and did not see them." At the time, my mom thought this was strange. My nephew explained that they traveled somewhere in the spirit during that time. Isaiah explained that the place they traveled to was like hell. This is why the police did not see them. When my mom called their names, they came back.

While living in the two different cities, my nephew was being controlled by two different witches. It was not just demonic forces controlling his body, but people who were participating in active witchcraft who were also controlling him. When someone sells their soul, they give up their own will, mind, soul, personality, and emotions. They take the deal that Jesus did not take. The devil offered Jesus the kingdoms of this world, if he would bow down and worship him (Luke 4:6-7). Jesus gave him the Word of God; we worship our Heavenly Father only (Luke 4:8). What does it profit a man to gain the whole world only to lose his soul (Mark 8:36)? Hard as this may be to believe, the human soul can be traded as a commodity in the spirit realm (Revelation 18:11-13). How can the Church win a battle they do not even know they are fighting? The good news is that when you pray in the spirit, the Holy Spirit is praying for the perfect will of God to come forth on earth as it is in heaven.

How did my nephew go from being trained to be in the demonic army to having his soul locked up in multiple places? How did my nephew get so demonized? He was not protected spiritually because of his parents. He was an open target for the devil. The devil used that teacher to introduce him to the idea of selling his soul. He learned witchcraft from that teacher and by playing demonic video games. The devil distracted the only intercessor in the family by playing on her weakness.

My nephew's father was in the occult, that is compounded generational iniquity. He had no saved father figure in his life. The enemy saw that he was called to be a prophet and decided to kill his destiny before he walks into his calling. My sister received a prophetic word about his calling while she was pregnant. The enemy distracted her with ungodly men and the things of this world.

All of this was a recipe for disaster, my nephew was chosen by the devil to shapeshift into a werewolf. The werewolves are occultic assassins. The devil has no mercy. If you do not obey him, he shows no mercy because he is the opposite of God. As soon as my nephew did not do what the devil said while being trained in the marine kingdom, he was locked up in hell and tormented. While in hell, he saw his older cousin being tormented. It was a continuous cycle of torment. The demons tormented her upside down. At the end of their cycle of torment, they would tell her that she was getting out of hell. Then, the demons would laugh and do it all over again.

There is a misconception that children do not go to hell. The Bible does not say that. There are children in hell, and their parents will be held accountable for not training them in the Lord. Babies are a different story and are innocent. I believe young children go to heaven because they do not yet understand the difference between right and wrong. There is an age of accountability, but that age is not specified in the Bible and can vary depending on the child and their life experiences. For example, I was 9 years old when I understood right and wrong. Therefore, I believe that was the age of accountability for me. This is why Jesus said suffer the little children to come unto him; for such is the kingdom of God (Mark 10:14). Do not forbid the children from coming to Jesus.

The moment my nephew was put into prison in hell, he was crying to get out. He said that the angel assigned to him would come often to try to get him out but would be beat up as well. Yet he would still try to get him out. I thought, "How is that possible that an angel of the Lord got beat up?" The angel that tried to bring the answer to Daniel needed the help of Archangel Michael to overcome the prince of Persia and Greece. Daniel's consistent prayers and fasting empowered that angel.

When God made the earth, he gave man dominion over the air, the land and the sea. Each one of these natural places also has a spiritual side. First, let's discuss the air. For instance, the 2nd heaven has a spiritual side that cannot be seen by the natural eyes. If Paul mentioned someone being caught up to the 3rd heaven, that means there is a 1st and a 2nd heaven. The 2nd heaven can be a place of captivity. My nephew's soul was split and then placed into different places. Although it may not seem like it, this is biblical. "Lest he tear my soul like a lion, rending *it* in pieces, while *there is* none to deliver. (Psalms 7:2)"

Let's discuss the land now. There is a spiritual side to what we see on the earth. The Bible mentioned that the earth "opened her mouth" and swallowed up Korah (Numbers 16:32). This meant that a gateway was opened from the natural realm into the spiritual realm causing the group with Korah to go directly to hell. Unfortunately, the fall of Adam and Eve allowed the enemy to occupy the air, land, and the sea. Jesus restored dominion when he went to the cross, however, the Body of Christ must enforce this dominion.

Let's discuss the sea. The spiritual side of the sea is the Marine Kingdom which is mentioned in the Bible. (Revelation 20:13, Revelation 18:21, and Revelation 16:3) When the legion of demons left the man of Gadarenes, they went into a herd of pigs. Those pigs then ran into the sea. The demons in the pigs were running back to the place where they came from. Adults, children, and even babies can be taken captive and held within the marine kingdom. The Lord Jesus wants to use his people to rescue them (Psalms 68:22).

I believe pregnancy is a very spiritual experience. From the time of conception until birth, it is a spiritual process. Every time life happens, the spiritual realm intersects with the natural realm. Therefore, babies can be taken captive if the mother does not watch and pray. While in the womb, John the Baptist was filled with the Holy Spirit. This happened when Elisabeth, his mother, heard the greeting of Mary, the mother of Jesus. If the Holy Spirit can fill a baby, so can demonic spirits. Pregnant women please guard your womb and stop letting everyone lay hands on your stomach. Also, guard what you watch and listen to while you are pregnant. I highly suggest listening to worship music and reading the Bible to your child while they are in your womb.

My other nephew, by the age of 2, had also been taken captive to the marine kingdom. I do not know if he was taken from the womb or shortly after his birth. Doctors would have labeled the child autistic. When my sister first arrived in Texas, all the children were demonized. The youngest one showed no signs of development; he did not talk, and if any word did come out it would be totally scrambled. He could not enter my home without being forced inside. He would not enter the door without screaming. He would often just lay down on the ground. He would not look at much of anything, he would just cover his eyes and cry. When his mother started going back to Church, he would just scream. She could not enjoy the service because she would eventually have to get up and leave.

After all the spiritual warfare with my family's arrival, I was tired. I dozed off to sleep while I was sitting on the couch. As soon as I dozed off, this 3-year-old child managed to find the bug spray I had hidden in my closet. The Holy Spirit instantly woke me up. He told me to run to the closet. As soon as I ran to the closet, I saw Melo attempting to drink the bug spray. I snatched it out of his hand. How did this child know it was there? We had to watch this child constantly; he would always try to run out of the house. When my nephew, Isaiah, came to after his deliverance he told us that he saw his younger brother in the Marine Kingdom. He began to share other experiences he'd had with us. He said he saw Satan pray to God and that when the devil spoke to God, he had to be on his knee s with his eyes closed.

Apparently, there was a section of the demonic kingdom designed for young children, kind of like a demonic playground. The demons would let the captured children play within that playground. My older nephew said the demons had evil smiles and looks on their faces. In the earth realm, it just looked like the child had developmental and/or behavioral issues, while in the spirit realm the child's soul was being held captive.

When we found this out, all my sisters began to pray for the younger child's deliverance. As we were praying specifically for his release, my 3-year-old nephew began to scream and fight. This child would not talk; however, the demon spoke out of my 3-year-old nephew, saying: "Mine." After about an hour, we saw breakthrough. His countenance completely changed. It was as if he saw me for the very first time. I could see the joy and freedom on his face. After this deliverance, he often wanted to come over to my place. He would come and sits by me at Church. If his brother bothers him now, he comes to me for help. He could now sit in a service without screaming the whole time. There are still some ways to go in his development, however, he now talks!

Chapter Twenty-One

The Warfare Afterwards

For a season following those days of active, non-stop warfare for Isaiah's soul, I had many more days of warfare. The arrows kept on coming, but God protected me. The process of my nephew's deliverance was more involved than I wrote about in this book. I was truly battling the gates of hell. It was like an alarm was set off in the demonic kingdom, especially when I entered a new territory.

At one point, while lying in bed, I experienced a night vision in which a woman appeared in the room. She had astral projected herself into my room. She seemed translucent, present yet indistinct, as though her form was partially obscured. I looked up and saw her overcome with rage, gripping a dagger and striking it towards me repeatedly. Despite her efforts, she could not touch me. There was something familiar about her features. Suddenly I realized she resembled someone I recognized from the Church I was attending! Astral projection is discussed in Ezekiel 13:18-21 and it is forbidden. God said he will judge those that do those types of occult practices. During astral projection, the soul or spirit leaves the body with the silver cord of life remaining attached to the physical body. The person can only travel the length of the cord and will die if the cord is cut.

"Or ever the silver cord be loosed, or the golden bowl be broken, or the pitcher be broken at the fountain, or the wheel broken at the cistern. Then shall the dust return to the earth as it was: and the spirit shall return unto God who gave it." (Ecclesiastes 12:6-7, KJV)

During this time, I also received several astral projection attacks from my upstairs neighbor until I found the source. She had demonic portals opened from her place to my apartment in several locations of my apartment. The one she had established in the bathroom was closed. Witches and warlocks love to enter the bathroom in places and do things. At the time of my nephew's demonic possession, they had used his body to open the demonic portal in the bathroom. I found this out through discernment and confirmation from prophetic friends that saw it in the spirit. I had to go to each location where a portal had been opened and pray in the spirit. I prayed for those demonic portals to close and did not move from a location until I felt a release. At the time that I was praying to close the portal in the spirit, my friend saw that the witch was doing everything in her power to keep it open.

While the demonic portal was open, I was extremely tired and lethargic. It was a fight just to stay awake. Water came from both the ceiling and my bathroom floor. It was so much water that I scooped it up with a bucket. My apartment also became infested with large ants that I had never seen before. The ants would come out of the sink. What in the world! I don't get along with insects. My car window also was busted out during this time and there was this strange sticky substance on my car that was hard to wash off. The warlock put a pumpkin on the steps facing my door. It was strange that their cat always watched me out of a window in their apartment. Halloween was not even close, yet they had a carved pumpkin outside. The carving on the pumpkin was ugly and demonic looking. Halloween is the witches' holiday. The warlock and witch upstairs seemed excited around that time, while at any other time they looked bitter.

After the portal was closed, the warlock that stayed with her poured a substance in front of my door. My doorbell camera caught some of it. After I saw that, I went outside and began to stand in that area and pray in the spirit. I poured anointing oil in front of my door. I anointed my place again and prayed as led by the Holy Spirit. When I felt the Lord's release, I went back in to the house. When the warlock got home, my camera caught him running to get that pumpkin from facing my apartment. Greater is the Holy Spirit on the inside of me than he that is in the world (1 John 4:4). Within a week they were running out of that apartment. I never saw anyone move that fast. I watched them move. They were gone within 30 minutes. Glory to God.

Another one moved in before long; she did not last long either. She couldn't even look me in the eyes. One night, two witches projected in at once. One came close to me and screamed and was then gone. The other one got closer and then she was gone. It seemed to be night after night, yet God gave me strength to endure during this season of extended warfare. It seemed as if these witches had nothing better to do with their lives.

The dreams I had were even crazier. In some, witches and warlocks were trying to feed me, shoot me, or inject me. One time, a group of them came at me, and it was one warlock with about 4 to 5 witches. One of the witches tied down my foot, another witch tied down my hand, while another witch was standing at the door watching and another was just standing there. All while a warlock was trying to inject me with some type of spiritual syringe. I said the name of Jesus, and nothing happened. I asked the Lord, "what is going on? Why are you not helping me? Why wasn't the Holy Spirit helping me to stand in your authority?" I didn't want to cut anyone's silver cord, because I knew that would mean their death. However, they were trying to kill me spiritually. God was waiting for me to take authority. I said, "I cut your silver... ." Before I could finish speaking, I heard their feet running away so fast. They all took off running.

I will share this one last dream that I had during this season. In this dream, a warlock showed up and he was so full of the devil. I thought it was the devil standing there. When he showed up, I went blind. I could not see. Later, I found out that God had sent an angel of the Lord to deal with him. The angel covered my eyes so that I could not see what happened. Once the angel of the Lord was finished with him, I could see again. Jesus was really fighting for me. When the Lord told me He was fighting for me, He knew that it was a network of demonic agents sent to take me out. I did not share all of my experiences in this book. Through it all though, Jesus was with me. I am still standing. My life is in Jesus's hands.

It is important to understand spiritual warfare is not always a sign you are going in the wrong direction or doing something wrong. The enemy was mad that I took my family off the satanic altar. I mentioned that all my sister's children were demonized. Unfortunately, there is still more work to be done. Jesus told the disciples to go to the other side of the sea, and they still encountered a storm (Matthew 14, Mark 4, Luke 8, and John 6). On the other side of that storm was a reward and victory. We shall see the rewards as well as victory in this life and in the life everlasting which we will experience with Father God, Lord Jesus and the Holy Spirit forevermore when our days here on earth are done. There is no greater reward than souls snatched out of the clutches of the kingdom of darkness and from the gates of hell. I have seen God send an army of his angels to retrieve one lost soul. The Victory belongs to Jesus; he just used me as his battle axe. If you belong to Jesus, you also have Victory over the gates of hell.

AFTERWORD

Time marches on and although no one knows the exact day when Jesus will return for His bride (Matthew 24:36), it is safe to say that we can all agree that these would appear to be End Times. Our fallen world seems to be approaching ever increasing alignment with the days of Noah when there was gross evil rampant on the face of the Earth. (Genesis 6:1-7, and 11-13)

When asked about the End Times, Jesus told his disciples: "But when you hear of wars and rumors of wars, do not be troubled; for *such things* must happen, but the end *is* not yet. For nation will rise against nation, and kingdom against kingdom. And there will be earthquakes in various places, and there will be famines and troubles. These *are* the beginnings of sorrows." (Mark 13:7-9, NKJV) As these things are happening currently, we are at the beginnings of the end times at a minimum. The same warning signs were shared by Jesus in the gospel of Matthew chapter 24, however, in this gospel Jesus continued to say that "as in the days (of Noah) before the flood" many people would completely ignore the warnings and signs of the times.

The pages of this book contain a very strong warning. The time has come where it is vital for us to understand the authority that Jesus has given us so that we may walk in dominion while undoing the works of our enemy, Satan. Through the testimony of the deliverance of Isaiah as well as his testimony of his direct experience, it is clear that Satan is busy training his minions for the End Time battles.

The Bible tells us that the bride of Christ makes herself ready (Revelation 19:7) for the marriage celebration. To prepare ourselves to be the bride of Christ, we need to walk uprightly, in integrity, as we follow the ways of Jesus and fulfill the great commission which He gave us. Jesus commanded us to cleanse the lepers, raise the dead, heal the sick, and set free the oppressed. He even took these instructions to the next level by telling us that everything that he had done was just the beginning or the starting place for us and that we would do even greater things than what he had accomplished (John 14:12-14).

We need to understand that because of what Jesus accomplished for us on the cross, we have the authority in the name of Jesus to cast out demons while also healing the sick. It is imperative that the body of Christ begins to walk in the authority which we have been given so that we can represent our Lord and Savior, Jesus, well during these End Times while also continuing to expand His kingdom wherever we go. We really do want His Kingdom to come on earth as it is in heaven.

If after reading this book, you noticed any evil patterns in you or your family's life. Please break those evil covenants and pray that every evil altar against you and your family be destroyed in the mighty name of Jesus. Before you break covenants, make sure you belong to the Lord Jesus Christ. If you are not a believer of Jesus Christ, first pray the **Prayer for Salvation** and if you need to break evil covenants, pray the **Break Evil Covenants Prayer**. Then, you need to be discipled. Ask Jesus to lead you to a Holy Spirit filled church, one that preaches and teaches the Word of God. Then, walk to the front of the church during the call for salvation and get baptized.

Prayer for Salvation

Jesus, I repent for all my sins. I forgive all those that sinned against me. Jesus, forgive me of all my sins and wash me in your blood. Jesus, I confess that you are Lord and believe in my heart you raised from the dead. I surrender and yield to you Jesus. Jesus, be Lord over my life. Remove my stony heart and give me a heart of flesh. Fill me with your gift of the Holy Spirit and with your Holy Fire! Write my name in the Lamb's book of life.

Break Evil Covenants Prayer

I repent for every evil covenant that I or my maternal or paternal bloodline up to the 5th generation established. I reject, renounce and denounce every evil covenant, that includes all covenants with fraternities, sororities, freemasonry, eastern star, elks, society of blue friars, Shriners, rainbow girls, job's daughter, or any other occultic organization. I reject, renounce and denounce all forms of witchcraft such as palm reading, Ouija boards, tarot cards, magic 8 balls, burning sage, using crystals, crystal balls, charms, witchcraft objects and jewelry, spells, evil eyes, curses, consulting with the dead, seeking out a psychic, being a psychic, wiccan, nature worship, voodoo, hoodoo, southern witchcraft, superstition ideologies, ancestral worship, yoga, new age practices, pagan worship, idolatry, rebellion, Luciferian worship, satanic worship, stubbornness, dark magic, and white magic. I reject, renounce, and denounce every evil covenant I made with my eyes by watching occultic movies. I reject, renounce and denounce every evil covenant I made by singing satanic songs, and playing demonically inspired video games. (Ask the Holy Spirit to bring to your remembrance anything else you need to repent for, renounce and denounce.) I take myself off the satanic altar. Lord Jesus, send your holy fire to destroy all evil altars with my name, picture, belongings, blood, hair, and/or any part of my body. Send your heavenly angels to destroy every evil altar against me.

I break and disannul every evil covenant and satanic agreements by the blood of Jesus Christ. Therefore, my pass agreements and covenants with death, witchcraft, the kingdom of darkness shall not stand. I am a new creation in Jesus Christ, old things have passed away, and all things have been made new. I am now covenanted with the Lord Jesus Christ. Jesus the mediator of that new covenant and the blood of sprinkling, that speaks better things than that of Abel. My identity is now in Jesus Christ, and I plead the blood of Jesus against every accusation of Satan in the courts of heaven. Every part of my soul be made whole in the mighty name of Jesus. Let everything that was stolen by the devil be returned to me, in the name of Jesus Christ. Thank you Jesus for salvation, deliverance, victory, freedom, and restoration.

STAY CONNECTED

Instagram: Sywithia
TikTok: Sywithia
YouTube: Sywithia
Facebook: Sywithia
Email: victoryoverthegates@gmail.com

Made in the USA
Coppell, TX
27 June 2026

83634381R00079